T0319021

Cambridge Elements ≡

Elements in Development Economics
Series Editor-in-Chief
Kunal Sen
UNU-WIDER and University of Manchester

GREAT GATSBY AND THE GLOBAL SOUTH

Intergenerational Mobility, Income Inequality, and Development

Diding Sakri
Independent Commissioner of West Java and Banten Regional Development Bank, Indonesia

Andy Sumner
King's College London

Arief Anshory Yusuf
Padjadjaran University, Indonesia

UNITED NATIONS
UNIVERSITY
UNU-WIDER

CAMBRIDGE
UNIVERSITY PRESS

Shaftesbury Road, Cambridge CB2 8EA, United Kingdom

One Liberty Plaza, 20th Floor, New York, NY 10006, USA

477 Williamstown Road, Port Melbourne, VIC 3207, Australia

314–321, 3rd Floor, Plot 3, Splendor Forum, Jasola District Centre,
New Delhi – 110025, India

103 Penang Road, #05–06/07, Visioncrest Commercial, Singapore 238467

Cambridge University Press is part of Cambridge University Press & Assessment,
a department of the University of Cambridge.

We share the University's mission to contribute to society through the pursuit of
education, learning and research at the highest international levels of excellence.

www.cambridge.org
Information on this title: www.cambridge.org/9781009382724

DOI: 10.1017/9781009382700

First published 2023

A catalogue record for this publication is available from the British Library.

ISBN 978-1-009-38272-4 Paperback
ISSN 2755-1601 (online)
ISSN 2755-1598 (print)

Great Gatsby and the Global South

Intergenerational Mobility, Income Inequality, and Development

Elements in Development Economics

DOI: 10.1017/9781009382700
First published online: March 2023

Diding Sakri
Independent Commissioner of West Java and Banten Regional Development Bank, Indonesia

Andy Sumner
King's College London

Arief Anshory Yusuf
Padjadjaran University, Indonesia

Author for correspondence: Andy Sumner, Andrew.Sumner@kcl.ac.uk

Abstract: In the Global South economic mobility across generations or intergenerational economic mobility is in and of itself an important topic for research with consequences for policy. It concerns the 'stickiness' or otherwise of inequality because mobility is concerned with the extent to which children's economic outcomes are dependent on their parents' economic outcomes. Scholars have estimated levels of intergenerational mobility in many developed countries. Fewer estimates are available for developing countries, where mobility matters more due to starker differences in living standards. This Element surveys the area, conceptually and empirically; it presents a new estimate for a developing country, namely Indonesia; it discusses the 'Great Gatsby Curve' and highlights the different positions of developed and developing countries. Finally, it presents a theoretical framework to explain the drivers of mobility and the stickiness or otherwise of inequality across time. This title is also available as Open Access on Cambridge Core.

Keywords: mobility, inequality, development, Indonesia, poverty

ISBNs: 9781009382724 (PB), 9781009382700 (OC)
ISSNs: 2755-1601 (online), 2755-1598 (print)

Contents

1 Introduction

In *The Great Gatsby,* F. Scott Fitzgerald sets the scene in Long Island near New York City in the 1920s. The novel's narrator Nick Carraway tells the story of millionaire Jay Gatsby who is seen as threatening to other characters as he is a social outsider, excluded from higher social circles of 'Old Stock Americans' due to his poor family background. Gatsby's rise is an analogy for the American dream of meritocracy – that any person can achieve a better life regardless of their background – though the story illustrates the fragility of the dream. Gatsby's story ends badly. He is shot for taking the blame for someone else's error. Although the novel shows people from low income can move up in society, it reveals the struggles and limitations that accompany mobility.

In the Global South economic mobility across generations or intergenerational economic mobility is in and of itself an important topic for research with consequences for policy. The study of mobility concerns the persistence of 'stickiness' or otherwise of inequality because mobility is concerned with the extent to which children's economic outcomes are independent (or not) of their parents' economic outcomes. Scholars have estimated levels of intergenerational mobility in many developed countries. Fewer estimates are available for developing countries, where mobility arguably matters more due to starker differences in living standards. In this Element we survey the area of mobility studies, conceptually and empirically; we discuss the 'Great Gatsby Curve' to highlight the different positions of developed and developing countries on this curve and make a new estimate of the intergenerational elasticity of income for Indonesia. We propose a new theoretical framework to explain mobility and the stickiness or otherwise of inequality across generations. The contribution of this Element is as a survey of the area of economic mobility and its relationship with income inequality.

F. Scott Fitzgerald's story has become embedded in discussion of mobility and inequality in the 'Great Gatsby Curve' (see for example, Corak, 2013; DiPrete, 2020; Durlauf, Kourtellos, and Ming Tan, 2021; Iversen, Krishna, and Sen, 2021a, 2021b, 2021c; Krueger, 2012; Narayan et al., 2018; Organisation for Economic Co-operation and Development (OECD), 2011), which depicts the relationship between income inequality and the intergenerational elasticity of income. The curve was introduced by Judd Cramer, a staff economist of the US Council of Economic Advisors and then by then US President Obama's Chairman of the Council of Economic Advisers, Alan Krueger (2012). Empirical depth was added by Miles Corak (2013; see also OECD, 2008, 2011). The Great Gatsby Curve posits that in more unequal countries, it is harder to do what Gatsby sought to do and move upwards. The curve depicts the relationship between the level of income inequality and the extent of mobility, proxied typically by father-to-son income elasticity. Various scholars have estimated levels of intergenerational mobility in OECD countries. In countries with lower income inequality, like Finland, Norway, Denmark, or Sweden, the tie between parental economic status (measured by income) and the adult earnings of their children is *weak*: less than one-fifth of any economic advantage or disadvantage that a father may have had in his time is passed on to a son in adulthood. Meanwhile, in countries with higher inequality, like Italy, the United Kingdom, and the United States, roughly 50 per cent of any advantage or disadvantage is handed over (Corak, 2013). In other words, the tie between parental economic status and the adult earnings of their children is *strong*. This evidence suggests that in relatively unequal societies, children of parents with comparably low income are much more likely to ultimately hold relatively low-income positions themselves. From a meritocratic point of view, this is problematic since it signals economic outcomes are associated more with parental background (e.g. class) than with individual effort and talent.

In developing countries, fewer mobility estimates are available, although mobility matters more in terms of ability to progress to higher standards of living above an absolute poverty line (Iversen, Krishna, and Sen, 2021a, 2021b, 2021c). There is literature on transient and chronic poverty (see discussion of Himanshu and Lanjouw, 2021) to build on that is typically based on official national poverty lines of governments, which, however, differ across countries in monetary value (both if local currencies are converted using exchange rates or purchasing power rates) and in regard to what is included in the consumption basket, amongst numerous other differences (e.g., Bane and Ellwood, 1986; Foster, 2009; Foster and Santos, 2014; Lillard and Willis, 1978; Ravallion, 1988; Rodgers and Rodgers, 1993; Stevens, 1999). Furthermore, existing measures typically require information on non-anonymous groups across multiple points in time. Such longitudinal data are sparse across developing countries (see discussion in Antman and McKenzie, 2007; Barrett and Carter, 2013; Dercon and Shapiro, 2007; Mckay and Lawson, 2003).

A major constraint – among many – for analysis of intergenerational mobility in developing countries is this absence of recent representative longitudinal data. Unlike (repeated) cross-sectional analysis which provides information about the income share of segments of society (and changes in their share over time), longitudinal analysis reveals changes occurring in the same household. If longitudinal data are collected for sufficient time to account for at least two generations (parents and their children), it is possible to estimate various measures of economic mobility across generations.

In this Element we argue the issue for developing countries – the Global South – is that generally developing countries are at the top of the Great Gatsby Curve (high inequality/low elasticity of income) before even achieving high income status. In contrast, developed countries are at the bottom of the curve. If there is a tendency for inequality to rise in the absence of counterbalancing policies during economic development, then the situation may worsen into the groups or classes of the 'privileged' and the 'trapped'.

The structure of this Element is as follows: In Section 2 we survey the field of mobility studies. In Section 3 we outline issues related to mobility concepts and measurements. In Sections 4 and 5 we review empirical studies investigating mobility in developed countries and then extend the review to developing countries adding a new estimate for Indonesia. Section 6 then turns to the Great Gatsby Curve. In Section 7 we outline a theoretical framework based on reviewed empirical studies and to identify determinants of meritocracy during economic development. Section 8 concludes.

2 Intergenerational Mobility Dynamics, Inequality, and Development

In this section we survey the meaning of mobility; the normative grounds to judge mobility, and the history of intergenerational mobility studies.

First, what is mobility exactly? Absolute mobility measures the extent to which children have managed to earn more (upward mobility) or less (downward mobility) than their parents, or to remain at the same level (stagnant/no mobility). It is generally the case that parents aspire their offspring to have better socioeconomic conditions than they themselves experienced. The spotlight on upward mobility is crucial. Downward movement may be driven, for example, by uncertainty and vulnerability to uninsured risks. Absolute upward mobility in turn is closely associated with sustained broad based employment opportunities, improved security against shocks, and income growth, in particular among the poorest population. Yet, the extent of absolute upward mobility depends not only on whether economic growth has occurred, but also on the extent to which growth has led to improvements in living standards among families from one generation to the next. For developing countries, it is essential to assess the extent that macroeconomic growth has passed through to income growth at the microlevel (households and individuals).

In contrast to absolute mobility, relative mobility is the extent to which adult children's position on the economic ladder relative to generational peers is independent of the position of their respective parents among the latter's peers. Relative mobility is usually interpreted as origin independence, meaning that the personal characteristics of the children (like talent, education level, etc.) rather than their parental background (like occupation, social status, or income position) determine economic status. This is based on the meritocratic idea that someone's life chances should depend on their own abilities and efforts rather than on who their parents were (Fields, 2005, p. 7). Origin independence has been linked with greater equality of opportunity which is widely supported as socially desirable (Jäntti and Jenkins, 2015, pp. 814–15).

In sum, both absolute and relative upward mobility are important for broad-based economic progress and for sustaining the social contract. In Narayan et al.'s (2018, p. 54) words:

> Without absolute mobility, living standards cannot improve, and social cohesion may be at risk as the different groups in society compete for slices of a fixed or shrinking economic pie. Meanwhile, a lack of relative mobility not only is deeply unfair and perpetuates inequality but also leads to wasted human potential and inefficient allocation of resources, which are harmful for growth. A lack of relative mobility over time, in other words, may constrain absolute upward mobility.

A question then arising is whether there are any normative grounds to judge any given mobility rate as good or bad or as optimal or suboptimal. Few authors discuss this, among them is Piketty (1995, 2000). According to Piketty, there is no a priori reason to believe that high intergenerational mobility should be considered socially preferable. Rather, the level perceived to be optimal depends on one's political perspective. Although categorising political view risks being misleading, Piketty nevertheless suggests that there are four basic perspectives on mobility.

The first one is the libertarian view, which tends to believe that public intervention should not interfere too much with the efficient functioning of private choices and contractual arrangements made by families and markets, even though this process might lead to little intergenerational mobility. Piketty exemplifies this view as the one exerted by Becker and Tomes (1986) given they interpret the level of mobility they observe in the United States as the result of moderately heritable ability and highly efficient functioning of the markets. The second view is that of the conservative right wing, which shares a similar view with its liberal counterpart regarding market efficiency but differs in terms of valuing the efficiency of individual/parental decision making. For Piketty this view is demonstrated by Mulligan (1997) who argues that persistent inequality and low mobility derive from efficient parental and market choices – in this case, high income parents who decide and are able to invest more in their children's human capital.

The third and fourth perspectives are left leaning, thus holding a basic premise that intergenerational mobility in an ideal society should be high. Such theories traditionally emphasise market imperfections and their inefficient, negative impact on intergenerational mobility. For the radical left wing, the third view, markets are imperfect, thus mobility is low and inequality more persistent than it ought to be. Hence, proponents of this view infer that the only possible remedy is the abolition of private property and the market system altogether. In turn, in the fourth view, for the liberal left wing, market imperfections need to and can be corrected because the distortionary costs of pure redistribution are relatively low. Supporters of this fourth view argue that opportunities for consumption and welfare should be equalised (through for example taxation) between to a substantial extent.

The central concern of research of intergenerational mobility studies, beyond such normative questions, is to understand the extent to which adult children's economic outcomes are independent of their parents' outcomes. One of the earliest documented signs of interest in intergenerational mobility, motivated by the desire to understand the rise and fall of dynasties, is the well-known *Muqaddimah* by Ibn Khaldun (1332–1406). This introduced the rule of four (generations) with respect to prestige, which asserts that prestige usually remained bestowed on one lineage for four generations. The four generations identified were labelled the builder; the one who has personal contact with the builder; the one who relies on tradition; and the destroyer (Khaldun, 1978, Chapter II, article 14).

Sir Francis Galton (1822–1911) was the first to apply statistical techniques to measure and estimate the correlation between parents' and children's characteristics. His interest in intergenerational transmission is documented in several publications from 1865 to 1897. In *Regression Towards Mediocrity in Hereditary Stature,* Galton (1886) studied the correlation between the height of 930 adult children and that of their respective parents. Galton found that children of shorter than average parents tended to be taller than their parents, while children of taller than average parents tended to be shorter than their parents. The child gained only two thirds of an inch for each inch the parents exceeded the average. In Galton's (1886, plate IX words: 'the Deviates of the Children are to those of the Mid-Parent as 2 to 3'). Galton (1886, p. 546) concluded that there was a 'regression towards mediocrity' in height. While the subject matter itself, height, might not be of much relevance to economic analysis, his technique is considered a foundation for modern statistical analysis in general, and for IGM studies in particular. He was the first to coin and apply the concepts of correlation, standard deviation, percentiles, and regression to the mean (mediocrity), which is a concept often referred to in the study of IGM (e.g., Becker and Tomes, 1986; Zimmerman, 1992).

Fast forward a century later, Becker and Tomes (1979, 1986) built a theoretical framework to understand the relationship between income inequality and intergenerational mobility. At the heart of their model are altruistic parents whose behaviour aims to maximise their utility function by deciding how much of their income they allocate for their own consumption, for making financial transfers to their children, and to invest in their children's human capital to increase the latter's potential earnings. It is assumed that children's endowments, parental investment in human capital, the rate of return to human capital (market), and government spending on education determine how much human capital the children will have, which in turn determines their adult earnings (see also Becker et al., 2018; Solon, 2004).

Becker and Tomes (1979, 1986), and Solon (2004) postulated four key determinants of mobility: (1) the strength of the 'mechanical' (for example, genetic) transmission of income-generating traits (heritability); (2) the efficacy of investments in children's human capital; (3) the rate of return to human capital investments; and 4) the progressivity of public investment in children's human capital. According to Solon, in a steady state, mobility will be low if (1) the heritability is high, so that genetic endowment-based ability offsets educational efficacy in society; (2) the human capital accumulation process is more efficient; (3) the rate of return to human capital is high, thus higher-income parents invest more in the human capital of their children; or (4) governmental investment in human capital is less progressive, so that credit constrained parents (most likely low-income families) invest relatively smaller amounts than their wealthier counterparts, hence the poorer stay poorer while the richer remain wealthier.

In addition to Solon's theoretical work, empirical studies have revealed further potential drivers of and obstacles to mobility which could explain the differences in mobility rates across countries. For instance, Kourtellos, Marr, and Tan (2016) and Chetty, Hendren, and Katz (2016) found that factors such as inequality, poverty, local labour markets, social capital, and local tax rates can potentially affect mobility rates. In the Element at hand, we are particularly interested in inequality's impact on mobility rates. As noted, the Great Gatsby Curve posits that higher income inequality tends to hamper mobility (e.g., Corak, 2013; Krueger, 2012; OECD, 2011). Consequently, in more unequal societies, children of relatively low-income parents are more likely to end up in a relatively low-income position as adults themselves. Against the backdrop that economic inequality is rising in many parts of the world (e.g., Atkinson and Morelli, 2014; The World Bank, 2015), this prognosis is troubling since it implies the likelihood of mobility will decrease if inequality keeps rising. In fact, empirical evidence on absolute mobility also suggests the likelihood of mobility is decreasing. The proportion of children who earn more than their parents in absolute terms is continuously getting slimmer. For instance, in the USA, approximately 90 per cent of children born in 1940 experienced absolute upward mobility and earned more in absolute terms than their parents did, compared to only 50 per cent of children born in the 1980s (Chetty, Hendren, and Katz, 2016).

The two perspectives (relative and absolute mobility) provide us with different aspects of the mobility story. However, approximate and crude, we should understand mobility better, that is, to understand its magnitude and scale, causes, and possible consequences. Then we may be well prepared to increase mobility through relevant policies to get closer to the normative characterisations of a fairer society.

The findings on mobility rates and their potential drivers may have important implications for redistributive policies. Piketty (1995) suggests that actual mobility rates, popular beliefs on mobility, and individual experience of mobility may explain differences in redistributive policies across countries. In fact, IGM has not only attracted the attention of scholars but also of policy makers. One important example is the Obama administration in the US, which viewed upward mobility as important, especially given the fact that inequality in the USA had been rising for decades prior to and during Obama's presidency. Obama's speech in Osawatomie, Kansas, in 2011 highlighted that the worryingly high inequality might have just broken the American dream that children will have a chance to fare better economically than their parents do:

> Those at the very top grew wealthier from their incomes and their investments – wealthier than ever before. But everybody else struggled with costs that were growing and pay checks that weren't – and too many families found themselves racking up more and more debt just to keep up ... This kind of gaping inequality gives lie to the promise that's at the very heart of America: that this is a place where you can make it if you try. We tell people – we tell our kids – that in this country, even if you're born with nothing, work hard and you can get into the middle class. We tell them that your children will have a chance to do even better than you do ... And yet, over the last few decades, the rungs on the ladder of opportunity have grown farther and farther apart, and the middle class has shrunk. (Obama, 2011, pp. 2, 5)

Obama's Chairman of the Council of Economic Advisers, Alan Krueger, then delivered a speech on the same topic on two different occasions. First to the Centre for American Progress on the 12 of January 2012 (Krueger, 2012) and then at the Rock and Roll Hall of Fame in 12 June 2013 (Krueger, 2013). During the former, Krueger used the term 'Great Gatsby Curve' to describe the phenomenon that 'countries that have a high degree of inequality also tend to have less economic mobility across generations' (Krueger, 2012, p. 4).

While to some extent the measures, drivers, and implications of relative and absolute economic mobility across generations within and between developed countries have been assessed, less is known about mobility in developing countries. One major constraint for analysis of IGM in developing countries is as noted, the frequent absence of representative longitudinal data. Unlike (repeated) cross-sectional data which give anonymous information about the income distribution (over time), longitudinal data shows whether and how the income situation of the surveyed individuals changes over time. If the longitudinal data are collected over a period long enough to capture at least two generations (parents and their offspring), scholars are able to estimate various measures of economic mobility across generations.

The World Bank published a report covering cross-country comparisons of mobility estimates in 2018 including poorer countries (Narayan et al., 2018) and later made the updated estimates publicly available in the Global Database on Intergenerational Mobility (GDIM). This database provides estimates of absolute and relative intergenerational mobility across more than 150 countries for 10-year cohorts born between 1940 and 1990. Depending on data availability, it also contains intergenerational pairs beyond solely father and son. Narayan et al. (2018) show that upward mobility is an exception rather than a norm. These findings underpin calls for public investments and policies that create more equal opportunities to narrow the gaps between the rungs on the mobility ladder, as we discuss later. Next, we turn in more detail to the issues of concepts and measurements.

3 Concepts and Measurement of Intergenerational Mobility

In this section we focus in greater detail on approaches to conceptualise and measure mobility following recent reviews of Fields (2021) and Iversen (2021). Mobility is a multifaceted and multidimensional concept. Therefore, studies are often not comparable conceptually or methodologically. Studies tend to highlight the seminal work of Sorkin (1927) and Glass (1954) respectively on the United States and the United Kingdom. Studies have made estimates of inter- and intragenerational mobility, absolute and relative mobility as well as educational, occupational, and income mobility.

There are various surveys on the area. Solon's (1999) literature survey on mobility elaborated intergenerational elasticity (IGE, β coefficient) as a measure of mobility within the framework of labour earnings and as a return on the investment of parents in the human capital of their children. More than a decade later, Black and Devereux (2011) updated the Solon survey to show numerous empirical studies applying the framework introduced in Solon's paper. However, as Fields and Ok (1999, p. 557) note there is no unified framework for mobility because the very notion of even income mobility has multiple definitions and thus different studies focus on different approaches. Other recent surveys include those of Björklund and Jäntti (1997), Corak (2013), Jäntti and Jenkins (2015) and the edited volume of Iversen, Krishna, and Sen (2021a), all of whom elaborate a frameworks, key concepts, measures and properties.

Fields (2005, pp. 7–14; see also Fields, 2021) proposed six different notions of mobility that apply to both intragenerational (changes within the same generation over time) and intergenerational studies (changes between different generations). Following this, intergenerational mobility can refer to: (1) origin dependence, which considers the extent to which parents' economic well-being determines that of their children; (2) positional movement, which compares children's economic position among their peers (ranks, centiles, deciles, or quintiles) to the economic position of their parents relative to the latter's peers; (3) share movement, which analyses how children's shares of the total income of their generation differ from the shares of their parents relative to their respective generation; (4) income flux, which investigates the extent of fluctuation between parents' incomes and the incomes of their children but not the direction of the change; (5) directional income movement, which is concerned with the number of parents-children pairs that move up or down and by how much; and (6) mobility as an equaliser of longer-term incomes, which compares the income inequality within the parental generation with the inequality within the children's generation.[1] In short, there are numerous concepts and measures of mobility. Consequently, as noted, studies differ in the measurements they apply depending on the mobility concept covered and studies are often not comparable (Fields, 2021; Fields and Ok, 1999; Iversen, Krishna, and Sen, 2021 b, c; Jäntti and Jenkins, 2015). In a developing country context, as also noted, intergenerational mobility studies are particularly challenging because of fewer longitudinal datasets and also because of the difficulties in estimating income where agrarian and informal employment are widespread (see for detailed specifics, Iversen, Krishna, and Sen, 2021c, p. 9).[2]

---

[1] See also Savegnago (2016) who summarises various indices of mobility including their formulas and references.

[2] One approach is that of Narayan et al. (2018) which is to use retrospective data on parental education in developing countries as a measure of intergenerational mobility.

We, in this Element, chose to focus on relative mobility as it is the most common focus in the area. Relative mobility measures the degree to which the economic ranking of adult children among their peers is independent of their parents' ranking relative to their respective peers. Relative mobility can be interpreted as origin independence (i.e., persistence), meaning the personal characteristics of children (such as talent or education level) rather than their parental background (e.g., occupation, social status, or income position) determine economic outcomes (as discussed by Roemer, 1998). This is based on the meritocratic idea that an individual's life chances should depend on their own abilities and effort rather than on who her parents are.

The canonical measure of relative mobility is intergenerational elasticity (IGE). IGE is usually derived as the least-squares estimate of the coefficient β in the following equation:

$$\log\left(\bar{y}_{i,g1}\right) = \alpha + \beta \log\left(\bar{y}_{i,g0}\right) + \epsilon_{i,g1} \tag{1}$$

where $\bar{y}_{i,g1}$ and $\bar{y}_{i,g0}$ represent the mean economic outcome of the children's and the parents' generation, respectively. Accordingly, $\epsilon_{i,g1}$ denotes all other influences on adult children's outcomes not correlated with parents' outcomes. The constant term α captures the trend in average outcome across generations due to, for example, changes in productivity, international trade, technology, or labour market institutions. The equation was first introduced in the context of mobility by Becker and Tomes (1986, p. 2) and is the standard economic model of intergenerational mobility (see discussion in Piraino, 2021).

IGE indicates the degree to which outcomes are 'sticky' across generations of the same family by estimating the percentage difference in children's outcomes for each percentage point difference in parents' outcomes. It represents the fraction of economic advantage that is on average transmitted across generations. In other words, β summarises in a single number the degree of intergenerational income mobility in a society. A positive value indicates intergenerational persistence of incomes in the sense that higher parental incomes are associated with higher incomes of children. In turn, a negative value implies reversal of incomes, manifested in higher parental incomes correlated with lower incomes of children.

Empirical studies in OECD countries have found β to always lie between zero and one. The higher the value of β, the higher the predictability of children's future economic ranking based on the observable position of their parents in the income distribution. The lower the value of β, the less 'stickiness'. In other words, when β is low, then parents' relative outcomes are a weak predictor of their children's future position in the income distribution of their own generation. Hypothetically, following Corak (2013), $\beta = 0$ represents a case of complete mobility where the outcomes of parents and children are entirely unrelated while $\beta = 1$ represents a case of complete immobility with the proportionate (dis)advantage of parents being mirrored one-to-one in their children's generation.

In the Eq. (1), both economic outcomes are presented in logarithmic terms. However, β estimations resulting from this log-on-log equation face two important limitations. First, the relationship between log child income and log parent income is nonlinear (See discussion of Sakri, Sumner, and Yusuf, 2022). This was not apparent in earlier empirical works due to smaller samples. As a result of this nonlinearity, IGE is sensitive to the point of measurement in the income distribution as shown in many studies (for instance, Björklund, Roine, and Waldenström, 2012; Bratsberg et al., 2007; Chetty et al., 2014a, 2014b; Corak, Lindquist, and Mazumder, 2014; Gregg, Macmillan, and Vittori, 2019). Secondly, the log-log specification discards observations with zero income which often account for a substantial fraction of the sample. Dropping zero income observations might therefore overstate the degree of intergenerational mobility. In other words, the way in which these zero income observations are treated can change the IGE estimate dramatically, see for discussion Chetty et al. (2014b) and Gregg, Macmillan, and Vittori (2019).

An alternative measure of relative intergenerational mobility which considers these limitations is the correlation between child rank and parent rank. This has been found to be almost perfectly linear and highly robust to alternative specifications (e.g., in Bratberg et al., 2017; Chetty et al., 2014b; Corak, Lindquist, and Mazumder, 2014; Nybom and Stuhler, 2015; Pekkarinen, Salvanes, and Sarvimäki, 2017). Thus, the equation above can be modified to:

$$\overline{PRy}_{i,g1} = \alpha + \rho\left(\overline{PRy}_{i,g0}\right) + \epsilon_{i,g1} \tag{2}$$

Let $\overline{PRy}_{i,g1}$ denote child i's percentile rank in the income distribution of children (generation 1) and $\overline{PRy}_{i,g0}$ represent the parents i's percentile rank in the income distribution of parents (generation 0). Importantly, this definition allows us to include observations with zero income in generation 1. Regressing the child's rank $\overline{PRy}_{i,g1}$ on their parents' rank $\overline{PRy}_{i,g0}$ yields a regression coefficient ρ which equals $Corr\left(\overline{PRy}_{i,g1}, \overline{PRy}_{i,g0}\right)$.

Fields and Ok (1999) pursue a rather different approach to that of Solon (1999). Fields and Ok argue that unlike inequality, mobility does not provide a unified discourse of analysis. They maintain that the very notion of economic mobility is not well-defined, resulting in different studies concentrating on different aspects of this multifaceted concept (Fields and Ok, 1999, p. 557).

Thus, for Fields and Ok, IGE as promoted in Solon (1999) and then by Black and Devereux (2011) is not the only measure of mobility. This line of inquiry was resurveyed and updated by Jäntti and Jenkins (2015). One handbook that discusses mobility is the *Handbook of Income Distribution* (see Piketty, 2000), which emphasises the theoretical model of mobility in relation to inequality.

In his extensive discussion, Fields (2005, p. 1) argues 'that the term *mobility* connotes precise ideas to various researchers, but it connotes different precise ideas to different researchers'. Subsequently, Fields (2005, pp. 7–14) proposes his six different notions of mobility that apply for both inter- and intragenerational (changes in the same generation over time) study as previously discussed. Further, given there are at various mobility indices, how should one choose a measure? The canonical measure of relative mobility is intergenerational elasticity (IGE).

IGE is derived from a regression-to-the-mean model, usually as the least-squares estimate of the coefficient β in Eq. (1):

$$ln\bar{y}_{i,g1} = \alpha + \beta ln\bar{y}_{i,g0} + \varepsilon_{i,g1} \tag{3}$$

where $\bar{y}_{i,g1}$ and $\bar{y}_{i,g0}$ represent the logarithmic form of mean economic outcome of children and parents, respectively in their own generations. $\varepsilon_{i,g1}$ includes all other influences on adult children's outcomes not correlated with their parents' outcomes. The constant term α captures the trend in average outcome across generations, due to, for example, changes in productivity, international trade, technology, or labour market institutions as previously noted. Hypothetically, $\beta = 0$ represents perfect mobility with the outcomes of parents and children being completely unrelated. In contrast, if $\beta = 1$, then there is complete immobility, implying the proportionate (dis)advantage of parents is precisely mirrored in their children's generation (Corak, 2013).

An alternative measure of relative IGM is the correlation between child *rank* and parent *rank* which has been found to be almost perfectly linear and highly robust to alternative specifications (Bratberg et al., 2017; Chetty et al., 2014b; Corak, Lindquist, and Mazumder, 2014; Nybom and Stuhler, 2015; Pekkarinen, Salvanes, and Sarvimäki, 2017). Thus Eq. (3) can be modified to Eq. (4) as follows:

$$\overline{PRy}_{i,g1} = \alpha + \rho \overline{PRy}_{i,g0} + \varepsilon_{i,g1} \tag{4}$$

Let $\overline{PRy}_{i,g1}$ denote child i's percentile rank in the income distribution of children (generation 1) and $\overline{PRy}_{i,g0}$ denote parent i's percentile rank in the income distribution of parents (generation 0). Importantly, this definition allows us to include zeros in children's incomes. Regressing the child's rank $\overline{PRy}_{i,g1}$ on their parent's rank $\overline{PRy}_{i,g0}$ yields a regression coefficient ρ which equals Corr $(\overline{PRy}_{i,g1}, \overline{PRy}_{i,g0})$.

There is no a priori reason to believe that the intergenerational transmission of economic outcomes is the same in all parts of the income distributions, which represents a clear limitation to the use of average IGE (Black and Devereux, 2011). A recent theoretical contribution by Becker et al. (2018) predicts that intergenerational mobility will not be constant across the distribution. This is partly because low-income parents are likely to experience credit constraints, while wealthier parents have a greater chance to invest more in their children's human capital due to higher returns to those investments. This will lead to higher intergenerational persistence at both tails of the parental income distribution.

Considering these differences in IGE across the parental income distribution, one alternative method to measure IGE is using the well-known conditional quantile regression (CQR) (Koenker and Bassett, 1978). In mobility studies, CQR is employed to estimate differences in IGE between parent and child outcomes across a conditional distribution of children's outcomes, as demonstrated by several authors (e.g., Grawe, 2001; Palomino, Marrero, and Rodríguez, 2018). However, this approach has a few notable drawbacks. First, the interpretation of the coefficients resulting from the regression is unclear since the pre- and post-regression rank order of children's outcomes is not necessarily the same. Second, adding covariates – which is not unusual in mobility studies – means that the conditional quantiles will vary across specifications. Therefore, the β coefficient resulting from CQR estimates has a different interpretation than that of standard OLS estimates in the sense that the former does not allow for a marginal effect interpretation of respective covariates.

Firpo, Fortin, and Lemieux (2009) developed a solution to this problem: a two-step procedure called unconditional quantile regression (UQR). Built upon the recentred influence function (RIF) regression technique they developed, UQR allows us to estimate the association between explanatory variables and quantiles qt (or other distributional parameters) of the unconditional (marginal) distribution of the outcome variable. This RIF-regression is similar to standard regression except that the dependent variable is replaced by the RIF of the statistic of interest, v, RIF $(y; v)$. In its simplest form, the conditional expectation of the RIF can be modelled as a linear function of the explanatory variables and the parameters, which is easy to estimate using standard OLS regressions. If the statistic of interest is the quantile ($v = q_\tau$), Firpo, Fortin, and Lemieux (2009) refer to this RIF-regression as an UQR.

RIF regression has been developed further by Essama-Nssah and Lambert (2015) to estimate the association between explanatory variables and a wide range of distributional statistics, including measures of central tendency, inequality, poverty, and the degree of pro-poorness of a shock- or policy-induced change in income levels. This method has been applied to identify covariates that affect poverty reduction (e.g., in Essama-Nssah and Lambert, 2016) and to investigate the causal effect of education on income-related health inequality (e.g., in Heckley, Gerdtham, and Kjellsson, 2016).

However, still only a limited number of publications use RIF regression in the context of evaluating mobility. One example is the study by Gregg, Macmillan, and Vittori (2019), who find that intergenerational persistence varies across the distribution of sons' earnings and is much stronger at the bottom and the top of the earnings distribution. In their empirical model, they changed the standard Eq. (3) to the following Eq. (5).

$$RIF\left(ln\overline{y}_{i,g1}; q_\tau\right) = \alpha^\tau + \beta^\tau ln\overline{y}_{i,g0} + \varepsilon_{i,g1} \tag{5}$$

This approach enables us to assess how β^τ varies at different parts of the distribution of earnings of the second generation. In other words, this allows us to understand if parental outcome has a stronger association with children's outcomes for those who end up being rich compared to those who turn out to be poor (Gregg, Macmillan, and Vittori, 2019, p. 508).

Given the strengths and weaknesses of relative mobility measures, especially β (IGE), researchers typically employ an additional, complementing concept, namely absolute mobility. Simple measures of absolute mobility are transition matrices; specifically, the quintile transition matrix which depicts the probability that a child is in quintile m of the children's income distribution conditional on their parents being in quintile n of the parents' income distribution. Transition matrices are useful in comparing mobility rates of population subgroups across the full distribution, just like the β^τ produced by RIF regression.

When estimating absolute mobility, researchers often group quantiles (e.g., Jäntti et al., 2006). However, Bhattacharya and Mazumder (2011) criticise this standard transition matrices approach for relying on arbitrary discretisation of the distribution (for example, quintiles or quartiles). They propose a new measure of mobility: the probability that a son's percentile rank in the earnings distribution of sons exceeds the father's percentile rank in the earnings distribution of fathers. In effect, this implies more weight is placed on small moves, as mobility is noted even if it does not involve the son's quintile (or other discrete measure) being different from the quintile of the father (Black and Devereux, 2010).

One statistic of interest in transition matrices is the probability of moving from the bottom to the top quintile (Chetty et al., 2014b, 2017; Corak, Lindquist, and

Mazumder, 2014; Dearden, Machin, and Reed, 1997; Neidhöfer, Serrano, and Gasparini, 2018). This is absolute upward mobility. This measure is estimated by the following formula:

$$UP_{\tau,s} = Pr\left(\overline{PRy}_{i,g1} - \overline{PRy}_{i,g0} > \tau | \overline{PRy}_{i,g0} \leq s\right) \tag{6}$$

In (6), just like in (4), $\overline{PRy}_{i,g1}$ denotes child i's percentile rank in the income distribution of children (generation 1) and $\overline{PRy}_{i,g0}$ denotes the respective parent i's percentile rank in the income distribution of parents (generation 0). Two important parameters in (6) are τ which refers to the number of children whose rank percentile exceeds that of their parents, and s which indicates the rank percentile that the parents belong to. These two parameters are defined based on the interest of analysts. If the probability of moving from the bottom to the top quintile is to be investigated, one disregards τ or rather sets it as any positive number and sets s to 20 (bottom 20 per cent), and $\overline{PRy}_{i,g1} \geq 80$ (top 20 per cent).

As an alternative to the previously mentioned conceptualisation of upward absolute mobility, the latter can also be defined as whether a child has more (upward mobility) or less (downward mobility) economic outcomes (in real terms) than his or their parents. There are two variants of this measure. The first is to compare the economic outcome at the same age between children and parents (e.g., The Pew Charitable Trusts, 2012) and the second one is to compare children of the same birth cohort to their respective parents regardless the latter's age (e.g., Chetty, Hendren, and Katz, 2016). The statistic of interest here is the fraction of children of the same cohort whose economic outcomes are better than those of their parents. Statistically, the unconditional probability that a child's percentile rank of earnings is higher than that of their parents can be stated as follows:

$$UM_{g1} = Pr\left(\overline{PRy}_{i,g1} > \overline{PRy}_{i,g0}\right) \tag{7}$$

A plethora of research has been applying these various measures to investigate mobility, albeit predominantly focusing on developed country contexts due to limited longitudinal data availability in developing countries. In the next sections (Sections 4 and 5) we turn to discuss these empirical studies in developed and developing countries and we add a new estimate for Indonesia to the developing country set.

4 Empirical Studies of Intergenerational Mobility in Developed Countries

This section discusses empirical studies of intergenerational mobility in developed countries. There are two strands of empirical research. The first employs international comparison aiming to determine patterns of mobility and, in some cases, their correlation with other macro indicators such as inequality measures and levels of economic development. The second strand comprises single or within-country analysis to understand dynamics of mobility (e.g., varying mobility rates of different birth cohorts) and to uncover potential determinants of mobility.

Jäntti and Jenkins (2015, pp. 856–63) highlight that researchers wanting to study mobility have to consider three 'W's: mobility of what, among whom, and when. The first one, 'what', refers typically to the income sources included in the definition of economic outcomes. Many variations are possible and definitions range from measures with only a single source (typically earnings from employment) to broader measures such as household income, which includes multiple sources. Mobility among 'whom' determines the income-receiving unit; for example, individuals with labour earnings. Benefits are assessed and income taxes levied on families and households. Recently, researchers have used earnings data for the children's side and household income data for the parental side (e.g., Chetty, Hendren, and Katz, 2016; Gregg, Macmillan, and Vittori, 2019; Kourtellos, Marr, and Tan, 2016). This is significantly different to previous generations of mobility studies that commonly used earnings data for both sides. 'When' refers to the length of the income period. Scholars often argue in favour of longer reference periods, assuming that temporary variations and measurement errors are then smoothed out, thereby providing a more accurate picture of living standards. Another temporal aspect of mobility studies to be clarified is the moment/age when the incomes of children and parents are estimated.

How researchers address the three 'W's is heavily constrained by data availability, which raises issues of comparability over time and across countries. Cross-country studies usually sacrifice detailed considerations given data quality varies across countries. Meanwhile, single country studies can go into greater detail, as data availability and quality of other countries do not have to be considered.

International mobility comparisons can be based either on collections of independently developed results from different countries (e.g., Blanden, 2009; Corak, 2006; Narayan et al., 2018) or on a full set of sample data for different countries, hence applying the same treatment to all data included (e.g., Björklund and Jäntti, 1997; Couch and Dunn, 1997; Grawe, 2004; Jäntti et al., 2006). Irrespective the methodology, international comparisons of intergenerational income mobility are complicated for at least two reasons. First, most mobility measures are highly sensitive to exact data definitions and data collection procedures. Patterns emerging from cross-country comparisons could reflect differences in data structures, measurement, and statistical approaches rather than genuine differences in intergenerational mobility. Second, as eluded to in earlier sections there exists no single objective summary measure of intergenerational mobility (Jäntti et al., 2006).

As we have discussed, there are two major mobility concepts, relative and absolute mobility. Both have been used for international comparison; however, the number of countries with relative mobility estimates is greater than those with estimates of absolute mobility. For instance, Corak (2006) and Grawe (2004) both included nine countries in their relative mobility comparison, Blanden (2009) has twelve countries, and Narayan et al. (2018) contrasted seventy-six developed and developing countries. On the other hand, examples of absolute mobility comparisons have involved six (Jäntti et al., 2006) or just two countries (Björklund and Jäntti, 1997). Next, a summary of both types of comparisons and the patterns generated from the studies will be reported.

Most international comparisons of relative mobility use earnings of sons and their fathers as the economic outcome and β (IGE) as the mobility measure. Recently, several countries have started reporting other copula such as mothers and daughters. The first wave of international comparisons investigated developed countries such as Sweden and the USA, most likely because data were more easily available. Corak (2006) compiled and compared seventy-two studies investigating eight developed countries (see Table 1, sorted by IGE from low to high).

There are a few patterns emerging from those studies, as well as contentions. It is evident form Table 1 that the USA is the most frequent context of mobility studies. However, the US IGE estimates demonstrate a common issue in mobility studies, namely the variation in estimates. Corak (2006) suggests this wide variation of IGE estimates stems from at least three reasons. First, sample sizes in the major data sets used (population study of income dynamics, PSID and national longitudinal surveys, NLS) are very small with only 100 or 200 observations or even fewer. Second, there is difference in sample selection criteria. For example, study number 54 in Table 1, by Zimmerman (1992), is biased towards workers in some labour markets in order to minimise measurement problems in deriving an estimate of permanent income. This implies that sample selection criteria may play a major role in explaining the wide variation in results. Third, the age when sons' earnings are measured varies across studies, which influences the degree of measured mobility. Corak (2006) proposes methods to standardise these problems in meta-analysis by using instrumental variables. This resulted in a more consistent estimate which suggests that IGE in the USA and United Kingdom indeed is relatively higher than in the other six countries studied (Corak, 2006, p. 53).

Table 1 First wave of mobility studies: the relationship between earnings of sons and fathers in developed countries (estimates of IGE of income by characteristics of study)

No.	Country	IGE	Age of son	Age of father
1	Denmark	0.082	40	50
2	Finland	0.086	30.2	45.8
3	USA	0.09	28	60.1
4	Germany	0.095		47.5
5	Germany	0.11	22.8	51
6	Norway	0.12	30–34	48
7	USA	0.13	24.9	53
8	USA	0.13	28–36	
9	Canada	0.13	29–32	42.5
10	Finland	0.13	34.9	46
11	Sweden	0.13	25–51	52
12	USA	0.14		47
13	Finland	0.14	40	44
14	Finland	0.14	39.7	45.7
15	Sweden	0.14	31–41	
16	USA	0.15		50.2
17	Canada	0.15		
18	USA	0.18	24–39	52
19	Finland	0.18	39.7	45.7
20	Canada	0.19		
21	Germany	0.2		51
22	Canada	0.21	32–35	45.5
23	USA	0.22	24–39	52
24	USA	0.22	28–36	
25	Canada	0.22	37.4	
26	United Kingdom	0.22	33	47.5
27	Canada	0.23	29–32	42.5
28	USA	0.26	40	45
29	Canada	0.26	32–35	
30	USA	0.27		45–50
31	USA	0.28	25–40	
32	USA	0.28		45–50
33	Sweden	0.28	30–39	43.3
34	USA	0.29	28–36	
35	Norway	0.29	40	44
36	Sweden	0.3	35–37	42

Table 1 (cont.)

No.	Country	IGE	Age of son	Age of father
37	Germany	0.32		
38	USA	0.33	23–37	40–45
39	USA	0.34	24–40	
40	USA	0.34	27–35	28–71
41	Germany	0.34		
42	USA	0.36	25–40	44
43	United Kingdom	0.36		
44	USA	0.37	28–38	
45	USA	0.39	28–36	
46	USA	0.39	25–37	
47	USA	0.39	25–33	44
48	USA	0.4	33	40
49	USA	0.41	28–36	
50	USA	0.41	25–33	44
51	France	0.41	30–40	55–70
52	USA	0.42		
53	USA	0.42	28–29	
54	USA	0.42	29–39	49.7
55	United Kingdom	0.42		
56	USA	0.45	28–36	
57	USA	0.45	30–35	27–69
58	USA	0.47	<46	40.2
59	USA	0.48	23–37	40–45
60	USA	0.48	32–40	
61	USA	0.49	40	46
62	United Kingdom	0.5		
63	USA	0.51	28–36	
64	USA	0.52	28–36	45
65	USA	0.53	25–33	
66	USA	0.53	22–55	43.1
67	USA	0.53	25–33	44
68	USA	0.54	29–39	49.7
69	USA	0.55	30–35	27–69
70	United Kingdom	0.58	33	47.5
71	United Kingdom	0.58	33	
72	USA	0.61	30–35	27–69

Source: Adapted from Corak (2006) and references within.

Some studies compare absolute mobility across developed countries with a similar method. For example, Jäntti et al. (2006) compare six countries: Finland, Norway, Denmark, Sweden, the United Kingdom, and the USA. To some extent this study is an update and extension of their previous study (Björklund and Jäntti, 1997) which contrasted only the USA and Sweden. In 1997 they reported interquartile (four-grouping) movement without a population-wide summary measure of upward mobility, whereas in 2006, they estimated interquintile (five-grouping) movement and a summary measure of absolute mobility. In the following paragraph, their more recent estimates of interquintile transition are summarised.

The sample used in Jäntti et al. (2006) consists of fathers and their offspring, both sons and daughters, from six different countries whose datasets were made comparable. Fathers were between thirty-five and sixty-four years of age when their earnings were measured, and the surveys were conducted between 1974 and 1980. The sons and daughters included in the sample were born between 1957 and 1964, depending on the country, while their earnings were measured between 1991 and 2001, again conditional on the country. The youngest off-spring was thirty and the oldest forty-two years old in the year earnings were measured (Jäntti et al., 2006, Table 1, p. 7).

Table 2 shows a complete list of interquintile transition matrices for the six countries included in Jäntti et al.'s (2006) study. For the purpose of comparison with the results of this Element later on, the table only displays father-son interquintile movement. In each matrix the cells of our main interest are highlighted; specifically, those showing transitions from quintile 1 (Q1) to Q3, and no movement but persistence in Q1 or Q5 by country.

Q1-Q1 signifies being 'trapped': prospects of staying in the low-income group are high for sons of low-income fathers. The probability of the 'trapped' per country is summarised in Table 3, sorted by preferred value (middle column). It is evident that the probability of being trapped is highest in the USA and lowest in Denmark. In fact, the probability of being trapped in the United States is distinct and much more pronounced than in other countries given that the lower, preferred, and upper bound values do not overlap with the values of other countries. Meanwhile, the probability of the other five countries overlaps, hence their ranking is not as distinctive as that of the United States.

Q1-Q3 indicates 'excellence': the prospects of moving to middle-income for sons of low-income fathers. The probability of sons to experience this kind of upward movement by country is summarised in Table 3, showing that the former is highest in Sweden and lowest in the USA. However, we should interpret the ranking in Table 3 with some caution given that the lower bound

Table 2 Interquintile transition probability of sons' earnings conditional on fathers' earnings: comparison across six countries

Denmark		Son				
(n = 59,213)		Q1	Q2	Q3	Q4	Q5
Father	Q1	0.247 [0.240, 0.255]	0.226 [0.219, 0.233]	0.194 [0.186, 0.201]	0.189 [0.183, 0.196]	0.144 [0.138, 0.150]
	Q2	0.208 [0.200, 0.215]	0.249 [0.242, 0.256]	0.220 [0.213, 0.227]	0.188 [0.181, 0.194]	0.135 [0.129, 0.141]
	Q3	0.188 [0.181, 0.194]	0.211 [0.204, 0.218]	0.224 [0.216, 0.230]	0.207 [0.201, 0.214]	0.171 [0.164, 0.177]
	Q4	0.165 [0.158, 0.171]	0.178 [0.171, 0.185]	0.204 [0.197, 0.210]	0.223 [0.217, 0.231]	0.230 [0.223, 0.237]
	Q5	0.153 [0.147, 0.160]	0.118 [0.112, 0.124]	0.156 [0.150, 0.163]	0.209 [0.202, 0.216]	0.363 [0.355, 0.371]

Finland (n = 5458)		Son				
		Q1	Q2	Q3	Q4	Q5
Father	Q1	0.278 [0.252, 0.302]	0.234 [0.209, 0.259]	0.203 [0.180, 0.226]	0.172 [0.150, 0.194]	0.113 [0.094, 0.134]
	Q2	0.192 [0.166, 0.216]	0.216 [0.194, 0.240]	0.249 [0.225, 0.273]	0.191 [0.168, 0.214]	0.153 [0.133, 0.173]
	Q3	0.177 [0.155, 0.201]	0.198 [0.174, 0.224]	0.219 [0.196, 0.243]	0.216 [0.194, 0.240]	0.189 [0.165, 0.213]
	Q4	0.164 [0.141, 0.186]	0.195 [0.169, 0.222]	0.195 [0.171, 0.219]	0.229 [0.204, 0.255]	0.218 [0.194, 0.243]
	Q5	0.151 [0.129, 0.173]	0.156 [0.137, 0.179]	0.140 [0.117, 0.162]	0.206 [0.181, 0.229]	0.347 [0.321, 0.375]

		Son			
		Q1	Q2	Q3	Q4	Q5

Norway (n = 26656)

Father	Q1	0.282 [0.272, 0.292]	0.234 [0.224, 0.244]	0.205 [0.195, 0.215]	0.159 [0.151, 0.169]	0.119 [0.111, 0.127]
	Q2	0.202 [0.191, 0.212]	0.238 [0.228, 0.248]	0.223 [0.212, 0.233]	0.200 [0.190, 0.209]	0.137 [0.129, 0.147]
	Q3	0.188 [0.178, 0.198]	0.209 [0.199, 0.219]	0.215 [0.204, 0.226]	0.210 [0.200, 0.220]	0.177 [0.168, 0.187]
	Q4	0.173 [0.163, 0.183]	0.183 [0.173, 0.193]	0.204 [0.194, 0.214]	0.221 [0.211, 0.231]	0.218 [0.209, 0.229]
	Q5	0.146 [0.137, 0.155]	0.135 [0.126, 0.144]	0.155 [0.145, 0.164]	0.209 [0.200, 0.219]	0.354 [0.343, 0.366]

Sweden (n = 31,996)

		Son			
		Q1	Q2	Q3	Q4	Q5
Father	Q1	0.258 [0.248, 0.267]	0.243 [0.233, 0.253]	0.215 [0.205, 0.224]	0.176 [0.167, 0.184]	0.109 [0.102, 0.116]
	Q2	0.209 [0.201, 0.218]	0.225 [0.216, 0.235]	0.237 [0.228, 0.246]	0.195 [0.185, 0.204]	0.133 [0.125, 0.141]
	Q3	0.183 [0.174, 0.192]	0.211 [0.201, 0.220]	0.219 [0.210, 0.229]	0.223 [0.214, 0.232]	0.164 [0.155, 0.173]
	Q4	0.175 [0.166, 0.184]	0.177 [0.168, 0.186]	0.196 [0.187, 0.205]	0.218 [0.208, 0.227]	0.234 [0.224, 0.244]
	Q5	0.163 [0.155, 0.171]	0.140 [0.131, 0.148]	0.134 [0.126, 0.142]	0.193 [0.184, 0.202]	0.371 [0.361, 0.381]

United Kingdom (n = 2205)

		Son			
		Q1	Q2	Q3	Q4	Q5
Father	Q1	0.303 [0.264, 0.342]	0.235 [0.199, 0.272]	0.165 [0.133, 0.199]	0.174 [0.139, 0.212]	0.122 [0.093, 0.151]
	Q2	0.241 [0.205, 0.277]	0.227 [0.188, 0.266]	0.182 [0.145, 0.218]	0.193 [0.159, 0.228]	0.157 [0.124, 0.191]
	Q3	0.188 [0.155, 0.224]	0.195 [0.156, 0.235]	0.227 [0.188, 0.263]	0.206 [0.170, 0.244]	0.184 [0.147, 0.221]

	Q1	Q2	Q3	Q4	Q5
Q4	0.161 [0.128, 0.196]	0.175 [0.139, 0.209]	0.229 [0.194, 0.264]	0.195 [0.155, 0.233]	0.240 [0.203, 0.278]
Q5	0.107 [0.081, 0.133]	0.168 [0.135, 0.199]	0.197 [0.162, 0.232]	0.231 [0.195, 0.271]	0.297 [0.258, 0.335]

			Son		

USA (n = 1798)	Q1	Q2	Q3	Q4	Q5
Father					
Q1	0.422 [0.363, 0.482]	0.245 [0.189, 0.302]	0.153 [0.107, 0.202]	0.102 [0.065, 0.142]	0.079 [0.047, 0.116]
Q2	0.194 [0.142, 0.250]	0.283 [0.230, 0.341]	0.208 [0.159, 0.260]	0.174 [0.128, 0.221]	0.140 [0.097, 0.185]
Q3	0.194 [0.145, 0.247]	0.186 [0.131, 0.241]	0.256 [0.198, 0.318]	0.202 [0.148, 0.259]	0.162 [0.111, 0.216]
Q4	0.125 [0.082, 0.176]	0.182 [0.129, 0.247]	0.198 [0.133, 0.263]	0.252 [0.198, 0.311]	0.243 [0.187, 0.300]
Q5	0.095 [0.057, 0.137]	0.122 [0.076, 0.170]	0.189 [0.135, 0.243]	0.234 [0.176, 0.294]	0.360 [0.296, 0.421]

Notes: These results include only those father-son pairs that have non-zero earnings. The numbers in brackets below the point estimates show the bias-corrected 95 per cent bootstrap confidence interval. Fathers' earnings were measured in Norway and the United Kingdom in 1974, Finland and Sweden in 1975, the United States in 1978, and Denmark in 1980. The sons and daughters were born in 1985 in Norway and the United Kingdom, between 1958 and 1960 in Denmark and Finland, in 1962 in Sweden 1962, and between 1957 and 1964 in the United States. Children's earnings were measured in 1991 and 1999 in the United Kingdom, 1992 and 1999 in Norway, 1995 and 2000 in Finland, 1996 and 1999 in Sweden, 1998 and 2000 in Denmark, and 1995 and 2001 in the United States.

Source: Jäntti et al. (2006, Table 12, p. 33).

Table 3 'Trapped', 'excellence', and 'privileged': prospects of intergenerational mobility by country

Country	'Trapped': prospects of staying in a low-income group for sons of low-income fathers: comparison across six countries			'Excellence': prospect of moving to middle-income for sons of low-income fathers: comparison across six countries			'Privileged': prospect of staying in the top for sons of top-income fathers: comparison across six countries		
	Lower bound	Preferred	Upper bound	Lower bound	Preferred	Upper bound	Lower bound	Preferred	Upper bound
USA	0.363	0.422	0.482	0.107	0.153	0.202	0.296	0.360	0.421
United Kingdom	0.264	0.303	0.342	0.133	0.165	0.199	0.258	0.297	0.335
Norway	0.272	0.282	0.292	0.195	0.205	0.215	0.343	0.354	0.366
Finland	0.252	0.278	0.302	0.180	0.203	0.226	0.321	0.347	0.375
Sweden	0.248	0.258	0.267	0.205	0.215	0.224	0.361	0.371	0.381
Denmark	0.240	0.247	0.255	0.186	0.194	0.201	0.355	0.363	0.371

Source: Adapted from Jäntti et al. (2006, Table 12, p. 33).

Notes: 'Trapped' refers to a son whose father is from the bottom income quintile and he himself is trapped in the same position. The value in the cells indicates the probability of that occurrence; 'Excellence' refers to a son whose father is in the bottom income quintile but he himself can reach middle-income (between the 40th and 60th percentile). The value in the cells indicates the probability of that occurrence; 'Privileged' refers to a son with a top-income father who stays in the highest income quintile. The value in the cells indicates the probability of that occurrence.

value of certain higher-ranking countries (e.g., Sweden) overlaps with the upper bound value of the next country (in this example, Norway).

Q5-Q5 signifies 'privileged': the prospects of staying in the top quintile for sons of top-income fathers. The probability of this happening is summarised in Table 3. However, similar to the case of 'excellence' in Table 3, the lower bound value of some countries overlaps with the upper bound value of the next country. Therefore, we should take the ranking in Table 3 with caution as well.

In sum, we can say that even in developed countries the comparability of mobility studies is a problem. In cross-country studies that can be directly compared there is an association between income inequality and mobility. This concludes our discussion of empirical studies of mobility in developed countries. In the next section we extend the discussion to developing countries.

5 Empirical Studies of Intergenerational Mobility in Developing Countries and a New Estimate for Indonesia

This section is concerned with empirical mobility studies focusing on developing countries. We add a new estimate for Indonesia.

Fewer studies investigate mobility dynamics in developing countries than developed countries due to longitudinal data constraints. The most substantial attempt at comparing developing countries is that of Narayan et al. (2018) who systematically compare mobility estimates for developing and developed countries using a consistent approach (see Table 4). As noted, the dataset was published as the Global Database on Intergenerational Mobility (The World Bank, 2018). Narayan et al. (2018) is a detailed extension of Corak (2006). The estimates of Narayan are presented in Table 4. It is useful to summarise. First, Narayan et al., note (this is corroborated by van der Weide et al., 2021) that the Great Gatsby Curve is valid not only for income but also for educational inequality and mobility; and that there is a mutually reinforcing two-way relationship between relative intergenerational mobility and income inequality. Furthermore, that higher levels of education inequality (school years of a cohort) are also correlated with lower relative mobility and akin to a Great Gatsby education curve.

Next, we add a new estimate to those for developing countries, namely for Indonesia. We do this not only to add to the set of countries with an estimate but also to demonstrate the issues arising in making an estimate.

The Indonesian Family Life Survey (IFLS) collects such longitudinal data for Indonesia since 1993 (first wave) up to 2014 (fifth wave). We use this dataset. The same data source, IFLS, has been used by Dartanto, Moeis, and Otsubo (2019) to study *intra*generational rather than intergenerational economic mobility between 1993 and 2014. They define mobility as moving in and out of

Table 4 Comparable estimates of mobility: high-income countries (HICs) versus developing countries (DCs)

No	Country	Income group	IGE	Cohort	No. of Obs.
1	Finland	HICs	0.11	1960	929
2	Denmark	HICs	0.15	1960	841
3	Belgium	HICs	0.18	1960	843
4	Taiwan, China	HICs	0.18	1960	695
5	Norway	HICs	0.2	1960	797
6	Germany	HICs	0.24	1960	1585
7	Kazakhstan	DCs	0.24	1970	520
8	Austria	HICs	0.25	1960	692
9	Switzerland	HICs	0.25	1960	778
10	Ireland	HICs	0.26	1960	1048
11	Singapore	HICs	0.26	1960	
12	Sweden	HICs	0.26	1960	722
13	Canada	HICs	0.27	1960	4193
14	Australia	HICs	0.28	1960	2463
15	Portugal	HICs	0.28	1960	748
16	New Zealand	HICs	0.29	1970	127
17	Netherlands	HICs	0.3	1960	912
18	Greece	HICs	0.31	1960	245
19	Slovenia	HICs	0.31	1960	608
20	Russian Federation	DCs	0.33	1960	672
21	Belarus	DCs	0.34	1970	433
22	Cyprus	HICs	0.34	1960	352
23	Guinea	DCs	0.34	1970	6314
24	Japan	HICs	0.34	1960	566
25	Kyrgyz Republic	DCs	0.35	1970	505
26	Ethiopia	DCs	0.36	1980	3353
27	France	HICs	0.36	1960	789
28	Romania	DCs	0.37	1970	379
29	Luxembourg	HICs	0.38	1960	
30	Korea, Rep.	HICs	0.39	1970	2416
31	China	DCs	0.4	1960	6117
32	Mongolia	DCs	0.4	1970	489
33	Macedonia, FYR	DCs	0.42	1970	432
34	Spain	HICs	0.42	1960	1001
35	Czech Republic	HICs	0.43	1960	1019

Table 4 (cont.)

No	Country	Income group	IGE	Cohort	No. of Obs.
36	Nepal	DCs	0.44	1960	2560
37	Pakistan	DCs	0.45	1960	5060
38	Croatia	HICs	0.46	1970	446
39	United Kingdom	HICs	0.48	1960	731
40	Vietnam	DCs	0.48	1960	588
41	Italy	HICs	0.49	1960	486
42	Uzbekistan	DCs	0.5	1970	627
43	Tanzania	DCs	0.51	1970	2131
44	Jordan	DCs	0.52	1970	3437
45	Bangladesh	DCs	0.54	1960	
46	Malaysia	DCs	0.54	1960	198
47	United States	HICs	0.54	1960	2214
48	Ghana	DCs	0.56	1970	7080
49	Chile	HICs	0.57	1970	15583
50	India	DCs	0.6	1960	19047
51	Slovak Republic	HICs	0.6	1960	599
52	Brazil	DCs	0.64	1960	4824
53	Nigeria	DCs	0.66	1970	2691
54	Kenya	DCs	0.67	1970	593
55	Peru	DCs	0.67	1960	5651
56	South Africa	DCs	0.68	1960	2526
57	Madagascar	DCs	0.69	1970	4435
58	Timor-Leste	DCs	0.7	1970	2897
59	Congo, Dem. Rep.	DCs	0.71	1970	0
60	Mali	DCs	0.71	1970	2799
61	Malawi	DCs	0.74	1970	1482
62	Rwanda	DCs	0.79	1970	3829
63	Albania	DCs	0.82	1970	420
64	Bosnia and Herzegovina	DCs	0.83	1970	482
65	Benin	DCs	0.86	1970	0
66	Tunisia	DCs	0.86	1970	1845
67	Bolivia	DCs	0.87	1970	1655
68	Latvia	HICs	0.89	1970	253
69	Egypt, Arab Rep.	DCs	0.94	1970	5791

Table 4 (cont.)

No	Country	Income group	IGE	Cohort	No. of Obs.
70	Morocco	DCs	0.95	1970	5055
71	Panama	DCs	0.97	1970	3037
72	Guatemala	DCs	1.02	1970	5154
73	Ecuador	DCs	1.03	1970	11599
74	Uganda	DCs	1.03	1970	778
75	Colombia	DCs	1.1	1970	7296
76	Sri Lanka	DCs	1.23	1970	657

Source: Adapted from Narayan et al. (2018) and references within.

poverty as well as transitioning from poverty into the middle or upper class, with the household instead of the individual as unit of analysis. In contrast, to Dartanto, Moeis, and Otsubo (2019), we construct a pooling sample with 9,445 matching pairs of children and their parents (thus individuals, not households) and compare their economic outcomes in terms of level and position in the income distribution (intergenerational mobility) rather than changes in parents' income over time (intragenerational mobility). Subsequently, two measures of relative mobility are estimated, namely intergenerational elasticity based on log-log regression of children's outcomes on their parent's outcomes and rank-rank specification. Furthermore, we consider how mobility differs by gender (of the child), and differs by generations. We find that although, overall, the intergenerational elasticity of income is low compared to other developing countries, the level of mobility in Indonesia differs markedly by children's gender and across generations.

To conduct intergenerational mobility research, one has to construct core sample pairs of parents and their children (two-generational copulas) or pairs across more than two generations. This first step enables analysis of the relationship between economic performance of parents and that of their children. However, the period of productivity of adult children occurs to a different point in time than the productivity period of their parents. Consequently, constructing such a sample is challenging since it must contain economic outcomes data for both generations. Previous empirical studies have used different data sources and methods to create such a sample. For example, Atkinson, Trinder, and Maynard (1978) traced children of families who participated in a survey carried out 26 years earlier. Out of 2,011 original respondents surveyed in 1950, only 1,363 could be traced by address and name and subsequently be mailed. This group of 1,363 traceable families was composed of 260 families who ultimately were not trackable, 57 who refused to answer, 220 who did not have children and hence could not be part of the mobility sample, and 826 families with a total of 2,236 children who could be included in the later stage of the survey to collect income data for adult children. Of these 2,236 children, only 1,348 from a total of 500 families could be located for income survey interviews. In short, after various follow-up surveys, the final sample eligible for mobility analysis consisted of 307 father-son pairs. As reported in Atkinson (1981), this great reduction is due to several factors such as excluding those fathers from the sample who did not work when surveyed in 1950 or equally those children not employed when surveyed in 1975–1978.

The method applied by Atkinson, Trinder, and Maynard (1978) is arguably better than a more straightforward method where both parents' and children's incomes are measured at the same time. The latter method, reported in Atkinson (1981), suffers from shortcomings such as limited comparability of fathers and children due to them being at very different stages of their life cycles at the point of comparison. Many children might not yet be independent of their parents, and even if parents are selected from older age groups, a sizeable number of children might have entered the labour force only relatively recently, which implies lower incomes in many cases.

A more desirable method than the previously mentioned two approaches is a longitudinal survey that encompasses responses from at least two different points in time that are sufficiently far apart to record income data of both parents and their adult children. An well cited research of this kind is that of Solon et al. (1991), who obtained data from the Panel Study of Income Dynamics (PSID). This is a nationally representative longitudinal survey of about 5,000 families in the United States that the University of Michigan's Survey Research Center has conducted annually since 1968. Solon's study focused mainly on father-son correlations in earnings, hourly wage rates, and family income with a main sample comprising 348 father-son pairs extracted from PSID. The sons in the sample were children from the original 1968 PSID households who, in the 1985 survey, reported positive annual earnings for 1984. The sons' sample was restricted to the cohort born between 1951 and 1959. Sons born before 1951 were excluded to avoid over-representation of sons who left home at a late age. The 1959 restriction ensured that the measurement of sons' statuses in 1984 was observed at ages of at least 25 (Solon et al., 1991, p. 397).

Another approach employs multiple administrative data to establish links between the children's and parents' generation such as in Chetty et al. (2014a, 2014b). The authors of the latter two papers constructed a linked parents-children sample using population tax records from 1996 to 2012 encompassing all individuals born between 1980 and 1993 who were US citizens as of 2013 and were indicated as a dependent on a tax return filed in or after 1996. The researchers linked approximately 95 per cent of children in each birth cohort to their parents based on dependent claiming, obtaining a core sample with 3.7 million children per cohort and 40 million children in total. Although this approach is undoubtedly powerful in serving empirical research, it is difficult to replicate in other contexts, particularly in countries where such tax and administrative records are not easily accessible for research purposes, which is frequently the case in developing countries.

In the context of Indonesia, the IFLS permits the construction of a core sample for mobility research. The IFLS is an ongoing longitudinal socioeconomic and health survey based on a sample of households which are representative of about 83 per cent of the Indonesian population and contain individuals living in thirteen of the nation's twenty-six provinces. The first wave (IFLS1) was executed in 1993 with individuals living in 7,224 households, followed by IFLS2 (1997), IFLS3 (2000), and IFLS4 (2007), which tracked the original households from 1993 and their split-offs, which by IFLS5 (2014) totalled in 16,204 households and 50,148 individuals interviewed (see for more details Strauss, Witoelar, and Sikoki, 2016). The original households of 1993 that had one child or more and could be tracked until the latest survey in 2014 were labelled as dynastic households. Dynastic households account for 80.20 per cent (5,794) of the original households and are distributed across all 13 provinces considered (see Table 5).

Dynastic households (5,794) are the source with which children-parents copulas can be constructed. The number of the IFLS respondents and the relatively long-time span of the survey (21 years between the first and the latest) enables the construction of a substantially sized core sample for intergenerational mobility analysis compared to that used in similar studies (See Narayan et al., 2018). It is possible to use all waves of IFLS to construct nine pairs: (1) fathers-sons, (2) fathers-daughters, (3) fathers-children, (4) mothers-sons, (5) mothers-daughters, (6) mothers-children, (7) parents-sons, (8) parents-daughters, and (9) parents-children. The complete list of copulas derived from IFLS is presented in Table 6. Note that the total number of dynastic households (5,794), which is indicated in the final row in the second column of Table 6, corresponds to the value recorded in the final row of column four of the preceding Table 5.

Table 6 shows the richness of IFLS data in the sense of how large the dataset is relative to the usual parent-children data used in the literature (see sample sizes in Table 4 from Narayan et al., 2018). In the IFLS, 5,794 households with 14,836 children represent our potential core sample for mobility analysis. However, this potential core sample only accounts for the fact that a link can be and has been

Table 5 Provincial distribution of sample: original versus dynastic households

(1)	(2)	(3)	(4)	(5)	(6)
Province	Original HH (*n*)	Original HH (%)	Dynastic HH (*n*)	Dynastic HH (%)	Dynastic/ original HH (%)
Bali	340	4.71	287	4.95	84.41
Yogyakarta	478	6.62	322	5.56	67.36
Jakarta	731	10.12	590	10.18	80.71
Jabar	1,111	15.38	872	15.05	78.49
Jateng	878	12.15	702	12.12	79.95
Jatim	1,044	14.45	796	13.74	76.25
Kalsel	323	4.47	262	4.52	81.11
Lampung	274	3.79	238	4.11	86.86
NTB	407	5.63	341	5.89	83.78
Sulsel	375	5.19	323	5.57	86.13
Sumbar	351	4.86	277	4.78	78.92
Sumsel	349	4.83	299	5.16	85.67
Sumut	563	7.79	485	8.37	86.15
Total	7,224	100.00	5,794	100.00	80.20

Source: Authors' estimates based on IFLS.

established between parents and their children without considering the availability of earnings data for parents and their children. We do *not* impute missing income data. Thus we use 8,889 pairs of children and parents and this sample remains representative of Indonesia.[3] This is a relatively large sample compared to a typical sample of a few hundred observations in the literature.

Table 6 illustrates that the longitudinal nature of IFLS data makes it possible to construct all nine potential copulas of mobility analysis. In this paper, the analysis first will focus on the parent-children copula type (type 9 or row nine in Table 6). As shown in Table 6, parents-children copulas encompass 14,836 children from 5,794 parents, which means we have a potential of 14,836 children whose economic outcome data may be compared to their respective parents' income data. The number of parents-children copulas actually eligible for intergenerational income mobility analysis depends on the availability of data to measure our main variable, which is economic outcome, for both parents and children.

---

[3] See (Sakri, 2019, pp. 70–81, 84–9) for full details. The details and complete steps of our earnings data estimation is described in the detailed appendix of Sakri, Sumner, and Yusuf (2022).

Table 6 All copulas of parents and their children derived from IFLS: potential core samples for mobility study

(1) Copula	(2) Dynasty (number of dynastic HH)	(3) Children (number)	(4) Mean age of child[a]	(5) Mean age of parent[b]	(6) Mean years of schooling, child	(7) Mean years of schooling, parent[c]
(1) Fathers-sons	3,949	6,937	32.67	44.37	10.70	7.17
(2) Fathers-daughters	3,818	6,433	32.53	44.02	10.73	7.24
(3) Fathers-children	5,119	13,370	32.60	44.20	10.71	7.20
(4) Mothers-sons	4,296	7,516	33.15	39.18	10.63	5.91
(5) Mothers-daughters	4,211	7,003	33.10	39.08	10.57	5.88
(6) Mothers-children	5,669	14,519	33.13	39.13	10.60	5.90

(7) Parents-sons	4,396	7,675	33.26	42.05	10.62	7.50
(8) Parents-daughters	4,307	7,161	33.23	41.91	10.59	7.47
(9) Parents-children	5,794	14,836	33.25	41.98	10.61	7.48

[a] Measured in 2014.

[b] Measured in 1993, age of older parent considered in copulas 7 to 9.

[c] Higher value among both parents considered in copulas 7 to 9.

Source: Authors' estimates based on IFLS.

In our estimate for Indonesia, personal income is used as the economic outcome. There are three steps to estimate the latter in this research. First, we define covariates of the income variable to be used in the estimation and imputation process in the case that earnings data cannot be directly extracted from IFLS. There are five covariates: working time, occupation, employment type, sector, and geographical location of the respondent's workplace. Second, we extract earnings data as reported by respondents and subsequently impute missing values in two cases: (1) non-reported salaries with complete data on covariates and (2) reported salaries that are outliers. The last step of our earnings estimation applies temporal and spatial deflators to estimate real values in addition to the nominal values reported in IFLS.

There are three issues concerning quality of the data, namely coresidency bias, lifecycle bias, and transitory income shocks. These issues should be considered carefully when creating the actual core sample for intergenerational income mobility analysis. We deal with these issues as follows.

Intergenerational mobility samples (matching parents and their children) constructed from household surveys are sensitive to sample bias (coresidency bias). This is because IFLS and other standard household surveys, such as the Living Standards Measurement Survey (LSMS) of the World Bank, usually include *only* the coresident parents and children. In contrast, they do not gather any information on family members who do not satisfy the coresidency criteria. Thus, according to Emran, Greene, and Shilpi (2018), coresidency restrictions result in a truncated sample. Since the pattern of coresidency is not random, most of the studies suffer from potentially serious sample selection bias when estimating intergenerational persistence in economic status.

One way to check for coresidency bias is comparing mobility estimates derived from standard household surveys as used in this paper with another sample of the same population (in this case Indonesia) that does not apply coresidency restrictions in the sampling process. However, to the best of the authors' knowledge, there is no such data accessible for Indonesia. Fortunately, the IFLS tracked all respondents longitudinally in all surveys succeeding its first wave in 1993 and updated the status of respondents' residence during each new wave. Hence, for each adult child we were able to identify the household s/he currently belongs to as well as her/his original household. In effect, we were able to not only create a pooling sample containing all the children analysed but also to use the coresidency status as control in our pooling sample.

In addition to coresidency bias, mobility estimates are sensitive to the age of both parents and children at the point in time when incomes are measured (lifecycle bias). Nybom and Stuhler (2017) show that intergenerational elasticity estimates can vary substantially with the age at which sons' (children in our case) incomes are observed, and that the bias is smallest when incomes are observed around midlife. When incomes are not observed around midlife, other researchers such as Deng, Gustafsson, and Shi (2013) as well as Ferreira and Veloso (2006) have tried to minimise the bias by including the age of the child and parent as well as their age squared into the estimating equation to subsequently compare the results with the baseline estimates. We followed this approach in our paper at hand. Additionally, we included a dummy variable for millennial children as a control. We define children as millennials if they were born in or after year 1980.

Moreover, mobility estimates are sensitive to transitory income shocks, which suggests averaging several observations of income at different points in time to attain results closer to the actual lifetime income than the ones derived from a one-time income observation. Therefore, in this paper, we average earnings data, after standardising them with spatial and temporal deflators, from a maximum of five observation points if data availability allows it.

Having completed the data construction process, the resulting core sample is summarised in Table 7. We find that earnings data for children are recorded on average twice out of possible five times compared to on average thrice for parents. This implies that the earnings data used for our intergenerational analysis is typically averaged from more than one observation for both children and parents, thus reducing the risk of bias due to transitory income shocks as the previous discussion outlined. Furthermore, Table 7 illustrates that children were on average 34 years old in 2014 when their incomes were recorded, compared to parents' average age of 43 years in 1993 when their earnings were registered. This indicates that both average ages fall within the productive age range, although there is a sizeable difference between them. This leads us to include age as a control variable when estimating the mobility index.

Our forthcoming discussion reports estimates of mobility in Indonesia that were derived from the pooling sample. The presented mobility estimates based on Eq. (1) were found to be robust to coresidency bias, lifecycle bias, and transitory income shocks. Therefore, they can be used as reference estimates of mobility in Indonesia. Table 8 illustrates β estimates for the three samples, which range from 0.291 (coresident = 0) to 0.326 (coresident = 1). This signifies that the non-coresident sample demonstrates higher mobility.

The difference of β estimates between the coresident and non-coresident sample suggests that children with higher earnings are potentially the children moving out of their parents' household and living on their own. This assumption is supported

Table 7 Summary statistics of the intergenerational income mobility core sample in Indonesia: parents-children copulas

Statistic	N	Pooling sample				
		Min	Median	Mean	SD	Max
Log earning, child	9,445	7.97	13.22	13.14	1.16	16.74
Log earning, parent	8,889	7.29	12.63	12.59	1.11	16.22
Rounds of data, child	9,445	1	2	1.85	0.97	5
Rounds of data, parent	9,445	0	3	2.80	1.28	5
Age, child	9,445	21	33	34.25	8.12	80
Age, parent	9,445	18.5	41.5	42.99	10.61	88
Millennials	9,445	0	1	0.56	0.50	1
Male	9,445	0	1	0.58	0.49	1
Coresident = 1						
Log earning, child	4,194	7.97	13.04	12.97	1.18	16.73
Log earning, parent	3,856	7.78	12.64	12.57	1.16	16.22
Rounds of data, child	4,194	1	1	1.66	0.89	5
Rounds of data, parent	4,194	0	3	2.67	1.34	5
Age, child	4,194	21	33	34.29	9.09	80
Age, parent	4,194	19.5	42	43.68	11.33	88
Millennials	4,194	0	1	0.57	0.50	1
Male	4,194	0	1	0.59	0.49	1
Coresident = 0						
Log earning, child	5,250	8.21	13.36	13.27	1.12	16.74
Log earning, parent	5,033	7.29	12.63	12.62	1.06	16.22
Rounds of data, child	5,250	1	2	2.00	1.00	5
Rounds of data, parent	5,250	0	3	2.90	1.21	5
Age, child	5,250	21	34	34.22	7.25	73
Age, parent	5,250	18.5	41	42.44	9.95	86
Millennials	5,250	0	1	0.55	0.50	1
Male	5,250	0	1	0.57	0.50	1

Source: Authors' estimates based on IFLS.

by the fact that median and mean earnings of those who moved out (coresident = 0) are USD 50.98 and USD 82.13 respectively, which are higher than the median and mean earnings of coresident children, USD 37.12 and USD 65.10.

IGE was also estimated by rank-rank specification (ρ) as in Eq. (2). ρ estimates (reported in Table 9) range from 0.277 (coresident = 0) to 0.313 (coresident = 1) and thus were found to be systematically higher than β estimates (illustrated in Table 8). Similar to the estimates of β, the ρ estimates of the non-coresident sample demonstrate higher mobility than the ones of the

Table 8 Comparison of IGE estimates based on log-log specification

β	Non-coresident	Pooling	Coresident = 1
EarningG0	0.291***	0.310***	0.326
SE	(0.015)	(0.011)	(0.016)
Lower bound	0.261	0.289	0.295
Upper bound	0.321	0.332	0.357
Constant	9.611***	9.245***	8.891***
SE	(0.193)	(0.139)	(0.198)
R-squared	0.075	0.088	0.103
N	5,033	8,889	3,856

Note: $^{*}p < 0.05$, $^{**}p < 0.01$, $^{***}p < 0.001$.
Source: Authors' estimates based on IFLS.

Table 9 Comparison of IGE estimates based on rank-rank specification

ρ	Coresident = 0	Pooling	Coresident = 1
EarningG0	0.277***	0.299***	0.313***
SE	(0.014)	(0.010)	(0.014)
Lower bound	0.250	0.280	0.286
Upper bound	0.303	0.319	0.340
Constant	39.665***	35.419***	30.891***
SE	(0.795)	(0.563)	(0.781)
R-squared	0.074	0.091	0.109
N	5,251	9,445	4,194

Note: $^{*}p < 0.05$, $^{**}p < 0.01$, $^{***}p < 0.001$.
Source: Authors' estimates based on IFLS.

counterpart sample. This strengthens the hypothesis that it is children with higher earnings who establish their own independent households.

How much do estimates of IGE of income differ by gender? IGE estimates (β) summarise the relationship between two generations at the mean value of their outcomes. However, according to Black and Devereux (2011), there is no reason to assume that β is linear for different parts of the children's income distribution. Therefore, it is necessary to check this nonlinearity hypothesis before continuing with further dynamics analysis. A recent theoretical contribution by Becker et al. (2018) on nonlinearity of parents–children relationships predicts that intergenerational mobility will not be constant across the entire income distribution. This is partly because low-income parents are likely to experience credit constraints while wealthier parents have a greater chance to

Table 10 Sample for gender difference analysis

Variable	N	Min	Max	P50	Mean	SD
Male						
EarningG0	5,163	7.94	16.38	12.62	12.58	1.10
EarningG1	5,452	7.97	16.41	13.43	13.36	1.06
DataG0	5,452	0.00	5.00	3.00	2.81	1.26
DataG1	5,452	1.00	5.00	2.00	1.99	1.01
AgeG0	5,452	18.50	88.00	42.00	42.89	10.53
AgeG1	5,452	21.00	79.00	33.00	34.09	7.87
Female						
EarningG0	3,726	7.29	15.66	12.64	12.60	1.10
EarningG1	3,993	8.28	16.69	12.86	12.82	1.20
DataG0	3,993	0.00	5.00	3.00	2.78	1.30
DataG1	3,993	1.00	5.00	1.00	1.66	0.87
AgeG0	3,993	19.00	86.00	41.50	43.12	10.71
AgeG1	3,993	21.00	80.00	33.00	34.46	8.45

Source: Authors' estimates based on IFLS.

invest in their children's human capital due to higher returns on those investments. This will lead to higher intergenerational persistence at the top and the bottom of the parental income distribution.

To check the nonlinearity hypothesis in Indonesia, IGE estimates from pooling, coresident, and non-coresident samples were tested using the RIF-regression technique.[4] In terms of gender and intergenerational mobility (or in other development processes), there are factors (e.g., social norms, discrimination practices) that affect the outcomes of women. Table 10 reports summary statistics of the sample split by gender (5,452 for males and 3,993 for females). The age gap between parents and their children appears unaffected by the gender of the latter. Additionally, the mean ages of both samples are around forty-three years for parents and thirty-four years for children. Age thus represents only a minimal risk for biased mobility estimates drawn from the split gender sample compared with those stemming from the pooling sample. The number of data points used for averaging earnings values of respondents is similar to that of the previous analysis, namely around three for parents and two for children. Table 11 reports differences in IGE between male and female children, both estimated by β and ρ. β estimates suggest that males have higher mobility rates than their female counterparts. The difference amounts to around five percentage points and is significant, as lower- and upper-bound estimates

---

[4] See Firpo, Fortin, and Lemieux (2009).

Table 11 Comparison of IGE estimates: male versus female

IGE estimates	β		ρ	
Gender	Male	Female	Male	Female
EarningG0	0.289***	0.348***	0.313***	0.310***
SE	(0.013)	(0.018)	(0.013)	(0.015)
Lower bound	0.264	0.314	0.288	0.281
Upper bound	0.315	0.383	0.338	0.339
Constant	9.731***	8.448***	34.718***	34.881***
SE	(0.163)	(0.224)	(0.743)	(0.865)
R-squared	0.090	0.102	0.099	0.098
N	5,163	3,726	5,452	3,993

Note: $^{*}p < 0.05$, $^{**}p < 0.01$, $^{***}p < 0.001$.
Source: Authors' estimates based on IFLS.

are almost perfectly separated. However, ρ estimates indicate that male and female children experience equal mobility levels.

In sum, our estimates of IGE in Indonesia add to the set of estimates for developing countries and do so with a much larger sample than typical studies. We find the IGE of income is low in Indonesia on average but there are marked gender differences. In the following section we situate our new estimate within the debate on the Great Gatsby Curve.

6 Great Gatsby in the Global South

In this section we turn to the Great Gatsby Curve. To recap, the curve shows the relationship between relative mobility in the intergenerational elasticity of income and inequality. Iversen, Krishna, and Sen (2021b, pp. 14–17) discuss in detail the curve and they argue that it may make more sense that the intergenerational elasticity of income is plotted versus a measure of the inequality of opportunity rather than outcome as they do as the logic to focus on inequality of opportunity is clearer in terms of link to mobility. We, however, have plotted in these figures intergenerational elasticity of income against inequality of outcome to follow earlier studies on the Great Gatsby Curve to situate our estimate for Indonesia and also to follow Kanbur (2021) who notes that there are positive and normative reasons to retain a focus on inequality of outcome. First, because inequality of outcome may itself be a determinant of intergenerational mobility. Second, that objectives such as the equality of educational outcomes are related to mobility.

In Figure 1 we present a stylised argument based on the empirical plots in Figures 2–4. In Figures 2–4, we depict the Great Gatsby Curve based on observations of father-to-son copulas (for consistent comparisons) IGE of income for almost sixty developing countries and 18 developed countries from the World Bank's Global Database on Intergenerational Mobility (GDIM) (2018 version).[5] We add our estimate of Indonesia's position in the Great Gatsby Curve enabling an international comparison of β. The estimates for other countries are comparable to those computed according to the three criteria. Namely, the same kind of copula, age, and economic definitions.[6]

We plot the IGE estimates for father-son against the Gini from the UNU-WIDER WIID Companion database (the Standardised, 2021 version). To plot inequality, we calculate the means of all Gini observations (or top decile share of GNI and bottom four deciles share of GNI) within the period ranging from year 0 (birth of son) to year 20 (when it is assumed the son is economically independent).[7] The dates of the periods were selected to include at least 20 years in the range if data availability allowed it.[8] Different colours are used to distinguish developed countries (high income countries by current World Bank classification) from developing countries (low and middle income countries), with the latter also being colour coded by region.

If we consider the set of figures we can generate a set of stylised facts are worth noting. First, the data shows that IGE is positively associated – in general – with income inequality. In short, a higher elasticity of IGE (which means children's earnings are more dependent on their parents and thus social mobility is lower by implication) is associated with higher income inequality.

Second, the data shows the preponderance of developed countries are largely situated in the bottom left quadrant portraying lower inequality and lower IGE of income. There are also several transition economies that are UMICs. Third, in contrast to developed countries, developing countries are situated in, or if not in then generally in the vicinity of, the top right quadrant, which represents higher income inequality and stronger IGE of income.

---

[5] The 2021 version of GDIM focuses on education and mobility only.

[6] See also Narayan et al. (2018, pp. 23, 141, Figure 4.2).

[7] Thus, in contrast to Narayan et al. (2018), we use the Gini and GNI shares for the period when the children were likely to be living with their parents. Other authors such as Corak (2013) employ the Gini for the year 1980.

[8] If no data were available for the year of childbirth, the earliest available year closest to 1990 was chosen, except if data were available for a year at most six years before the birth year and the available post-birth year was more than twice as far from the birth year than the available pre-birth year.

		Income inequality	
		Lower	Higher
IGE of income (father to son)	Higher		Developing countries
	Lower	Developed countries (HICs) plus transition economies	

Figure 1 Four quadrants illustrating the *stylised* relationship between IGE of income and income inequality

Source: Authors' elaboration.

In other words, with few notable exceptions, the values in the Great Gatsby Curve Figure 2 shows that developed countries exhibit higher mobility and less inequality, and that the opposed is true, in general, for developing countries. Among developed countries (dark blue–coloured plots), the United States, Slovakia, and Latvia are outliers exhibiting deviation in one or both indicators. Indonesia, when our estimate is added, and Kazakhstan are two exceptions for developing countries as they have lower IGE.

Furthermore, when we plot a (linear) line of best fit that line is higher for the developing countries group compared to the line of best fit (linear) for the developed countries group. In other words, if we take those lines then at any given level of income inequality the IGE of income is likely to be higher (and thus mobility worse) in a developing country than in a developed country.[9]

Figures 3 and 4 respectively show the IGE versus the top decile share of income and bottom four decile share of income. Figure 3 follows a similar pattern to Figure 2. In Figure 4, the pattern is inverted as the data are depicting the income share of the bottom 40 per cent of the population.

In sum, with caveats, an association between IGE and income inequality is clear enough. Further, countries tend to be segregated into two groups: developed countries (High-Income Countries) with lower income inequality and lower IGE of

---

[9] Narayan et al. (2018, p. 114) also present linear plots using the GDIM database and separating developing economies and high-income countries using the 1960s cohort, IGE of income and '2000s data' for the Gini drawn from World Development Indicators rather than UNU-WIDER WIID Companion. There is only a cursory discussion of the data figure where it is noted that the correlation (of IGE of income to inequality) is stronger (the curve is steeper curve) in developing countries than HICs.

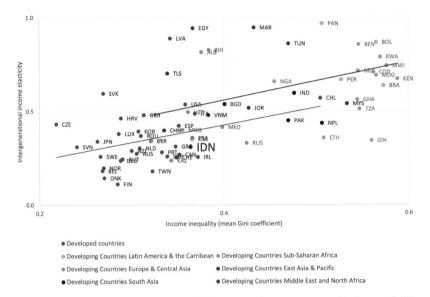

Figure 2 IGE of income elasticity (father-to-son) versus mean Gini, year 0–20: developed countries (blue line of best fit) versus developing countries (red line of best fit)

Note: Classification into developing/developed country according to World Bank current income group classification (HIC/non-HIC). Three outliers are not plotted on the figure (Colombia; Sri Lanka; South Africa).

Source: Authors' estimates based on World Bank GDIM (2018) and UNU-WIDER (2021) WIID Companion. Indonesia estimate based authors' calculation using IFLS (father-son copulas from the birth cohort 1970).

income and conversely, developing countries with – in general – higher income inequality and higher IGE of income. Further research is needed on this matter as it implies a redistribution imperative in developing countries to achieve fairer societies. Iversen, Krishna, and Sen (2021a, pp. 18–19) argue that developing countries may be different to developed countries in terms of the Great Gatsby Curve because of shifts in the patterns of structural transformation from the earlier pathway of an agriculture to manufacturing labour movement to a more recent pattern of agriculture to low productivity services (as empirically identified by Baymul and Sen, 2020).

Does Indonesia buck the trend? Indonesia does have a lower IGE than typical developing countries. On the other hand, Indonesia is a good example of declining IGE with rising income inequality. In other words, a within-country Great Gatsby Curve rather than a cross-country curve (see discussion in DiPrete, 2020). Although Indonesia has a low IGE it has been worsening over time as income inequality has risen (see Yusuf, Sumner, and Rum, 2014). In Table 12 we estimate a significant

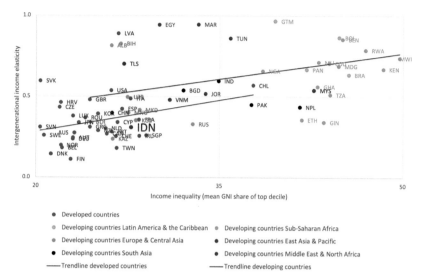

Figure 3 IGE of income elasticity (father-to-son) versus mean share of GNI to top decile, year 0–20: developed countries (blue line of best fit) versus developing countries (red line of best fit)

Note: Classification into developing/developed country according to World Bank current income group classification (HIC/non-HIC). Three outliers are not plotted on the figure (Colombia; Sri Lanka; South Africa).

Source: Authors' estimates based on World Bank GDIM (2018) and UNU-WIDER (2021) WIID Companion. Indonesia estimate based on authors' calculation using IFLS (father-son copulas from the birth cohort 1970).

Table 12 Comparison of IGE estimates for Indonesia: pre-millennials versus millennials

IGE estimates	β		ρ	
Generation	Pre-millennials	Millennials	Pre-millennials	Millennials
EarningG0	0.264***	0.337***	0.249***	0.324***
SE	(0.016)	(0.017)	(0.015)	(0.015)
Lower bound	0.232	0.305	0.220	0.295
Upper bound	0.295	0.370	0.277	0.354
Constant	9.773***	8.928***	36.278***	34.857***
SE	(0.195)	(0.213)	(0.703)	(0.956)
R-squared	0.075	0.082	0.068	0.084
N	3644	5245	4153	5292

Note: $^{*}p < 0.05$, $^{**}p < 0.01$, $^{***}p < 0.001$.
Source: Authors' estimate based on IFLS.

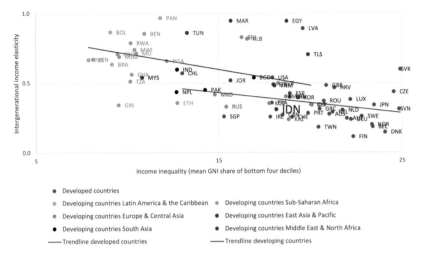

Figure 4 IGE of income elasticity (father-to-son) versus mean share of GNI to poorest two quintiles, year 0–20: developed countries (blue line of best fit) versus developing countries (red line of best fit)

Note: Classification into developing/developed country according to World Bank current income group classification (HIC/non-HIC). Three outliers are not plotted on the figure (Colombia; Sri Lanka; South Africa).

Source: Authors' estimates based on World Bank GDIM (2018) and UNU-WIDER (2021) WIID Companion. Indonesia estimate based on authors' calculation using IFLS (father-son copulas from the birth cohort 1970).

difference between pre-millennials' and millennials' mobility rates. According to β estimates (second and third row), at 95 per cent confidence interval, the lower and upper bound of the two groups are clearly far apart. This gives us confidence to infer that the mobility rate is declining by a factor of around seven percentage points when comparing pre-millennials with millennials. This conclusion is supported by rank-rank specification estimates, ρ (fourth and fifth row). It was shown in the previous section that ρ yields lower estimates of IGE than β. Hence, it should not be surprising that ρ estimates are lower than β estimates for both ends. However, the most important insight from ρ in this case is that it corroborates a difference in mobility rates of pre-millennials and millennials.

A possible cause of this decline in mobility is the age difference between the two groups at the moment of measurement. Although it has been mentioned that the mobility estimates are assumed to have minimal lifecycle bias since the mean age of the children was mature enough when their earnings were measured, the effect might still become apparent. Thirteen years of difference between pre-millennials and millennials could possibly mean that the former (41.5 years old on average) are approaching the income peak of their working life whereas the latter

Table 13 Age-adjusted comparison of IGE estimates for Indonesia:
pre-millennials versus millennials

IGE estimates	β		ρ	
Generation	Pre-millennials	Millennials	Pre-millennials	Millennials
EarningG0	0.262***	0.340***	0.250***	0.325***
SE	(0.018)	(0.018)	(0.017)	(0.016)
Lower bound	0.227	0.306	0.217	0.294
Upper bound	0.297	0.374	0.283	0.356
AgeG0	0.021	0.067***	0.766*	1.687***
SE	(0.021)	(0.015)	(0.391)	(0.369)
SqAgeG0	−0.000	−0.001***	−0.007	−0.018***
SE	(0.000)	(0.000)	(0.004)	(0.005)
AgeG1	0.049	0.094	1.971***	1.680
SE	(0.038)	(0.063)	(0.551)	(1.566)
SqAgeG1	−0.001	−0.002*	−0.022***	−0.046
SE	(0.000)	(0.001)	(0.006)	(0.028)
Constant	8.236***	6.609***	−26.640*	−11.763
SE	(0.858)	(0.907)	(12.917)	(22.008)
R-squared	0.075	0.091	0.073	0.095
N	3644	5245	4153	5292

Note: $^{*} p < 0.05$, $^{**} p < 0.01$, $^{***} p < 0.001$.
Source: Authors' estimate based on IFLS.

(28.5 years of age) are in earlier stages of their working life. Likewise, the parents of millennials (mean age 37.4) might be at their peak whereas the productivity of the parents of pre-millennials (50.1) might be post-peak.

To assess the effect of age on mobility estimates, this research follows other studies such as Deng, Gustafsson, and Shi (2013) and Ferreira and Veloso (2006). Consequently, we include age and squared age of both children and parents in Eqs. (1) and (2) introduced earlier in this paper. Table 13 reports the results and illustrates that age of neither parents nor children affects mobility estimates, irrespective of whether β or ρ is measured. Furthermore, the difference between pre-millennials and millennials remains approximately the same, which means the former experience lower IGE (higher mobility) than the latter. This implies that the findings of declining mobility rates between pre-millennials and millennials most likely do not stem from data construction.

In sum, if we situate Indonesia within the Great Gatsby Curve it has a lower IGE compared to most developing countries. However, not only are there gender differences previously highlighted, Indonesia's IGE has fallen over time as income inequality has risen suggesting a *within-country* Great Gatsby Curve.

Overall, across countries with just a few exceptions, we observe that the IGE of income is higher for developing countries and lower for high-income countries. Exceptions include the USA (a developed country) and Indonesia (a developing country). If developing countries are already at the wrong end of the curve before reaching higher-income levels comparable to those of developed countries and if there is a tendency for gross income inequality to rise during structural transformation, at least in the absence of public policy interventions, then the situation in developing countries is likely to worsen into solidified groups of the 'privileged' and the 'trapped'. Thus, anything less than substantially low inequality might not suffice to eliminate this 'class ceiling' of privilege at the top and the trappedness in the bottom 'class'. In the next section we present a theoretical framework to understand the inequality–mobility-development relationship.

7 A Theoretical Framework for Understanding Intergenerational Mobility Dynamics, Inequality, and Development

In this section we discuss the relationship between mobility, inequality and development. Several within-country studies have investigated drivers of inter-generational mobility (see for a summary discussion in Iversen, Krishna, and Sen, 2021c, p. 453; and for in-depth discussion, see Piraino, 2021, pp. 39–49). For instance Kourtellos, Marr, and Tan (2016) or Chetty et al. (2014b) reveal a strong correlation between mobility and several covariates acting as potential determinants of intergenerational mobility. For example, Chetty et al. (2014b) use tax income data of both the children's and parents' generations with a sample size of more than 40 million children and their parents. To identify potential determinants of mobility, they disaggregate their data by subnational level.

Becker and Tomes (1979, 1986) were the first to build a theoretical framework of intergenerational mobility, which is related to inequality but differs in economic outcome. At that time, theoretical concepts, methodological measures, and empirical evidence of inequality were not always considered part of economics. Shorrocks (1978) is one example of building theory connecting inequality and intragenerational mobility at that time.

At the heart of Becker and Tomes' model are altruistic parents whose goal is to maximise their utility function by deciding how much of their income they allocate for own consumption, for financial transfers to their children, and for investments in their children's human capital to spur the latter's potential earnings. It is assumed that children's endowments, parental investment in human capital, and the rate of return to human capital (the market) determine how much human capital the children will have, which in turn determines their adult earnings.

According to Solon (1999), based on Becker and Tomes (1979), intergenerational transmission of advantages occurs both because higher-earning parents invest more in their children's human capital and because children of such parents tend to have higher endowments arising from genetics or from environmental influences during childhood. More recently, Solon (2004) expanded his model to allow for governmental investment in children's human capital that may be progressive in the sense that the ratio of government investment to parental income decreases with parental income. This model implies that intergenerational elasticity is increased by the heritability of earnings-related endowments and the rate of return to human capital investments but decreased by the progressivity of government investments.

We can develop a contemporary theoretical framework based on the *empirical* studies in high income and developing countries which show that the overlapping, *main* determinants of intergenerational income mobility are generally inequality-related with a cross-cutting theme of economic dualism in terms of structural transformation. This builds on the summary of Iversen, Krishna, and Sen (2021c, pp. 453–8) in both the list of drivers (or groupings) and public policies required that each driver implies and Piraino (2021, pp. 39–49), (who focuses three drivers in particular: labour market segmentation, credit and risk failures and information frictions which overlap with some of the forthcoming discussion).

We can specify three domains: First, overall levels of and trends in income inequality of outcome and opportunity. Second, segregation by race and class. Third, quantitative and qualitative public investments in education. Fourth, the stability of GNI capture by the 'middle'. Finally, cross-cutting these set of issues is the question of economic dualism.

There are of course various other issues we could add. For example, as developing countries become more urbanised with a rising services sector, the wage premium for particular skills (e.g., high-end finance and many other urban services) is rising, contributing to increasing inequality (also with spatial and gender dimensions). Then there are the many aspects of tax and transfer regimes, including generally weak progressivity in the tax system (capital especially lightly taxed), and limited, sometimes poorly targeted social transfers.

First, overall levels of and trends in the inequality of both outcome and opportunities: As noted studies have identified a negative correlation between income inequality and intergenerational mobility across countries. Chetty et al. (2014b) explore whether there is an analogous relationship across areas within the United States by correlating upward mobility with the Gini coefficient of parents' income within each commuting zone. They conclude there is a robust negative correlation between inequality within the current generation of adults and mobility across generations. Intuitively, inequality of opportunity ought to be associated with social mobility and changes in inequality of opportunity would have consequences for social mobility. Further, inequality of outcome ought to be associated with social mobility for the reasons identified by Kanbur (2021), specifically that one generations inequality of outcome is the next generations inequality of opportunity. DiPrete (2020, pp. 385–9) discusses in depth the four types of evidence that have been used to evaluate the inequality–mobility relationship: Across country; within-country over time; correlation through mechanisms that connect the position of parents and their offspring and natural experiments and concludes that although proving that inequality determines mobility is complex, the forces that cause inequality to rise are also lowering mobility.

Second, segregation by race and class: Two measures of segregation have been investigated, namely racial and poverty segregation. Scholars find that areas with large black populations have lower rates of upward mobility for children of all races. There are many potential mechanisms for such a correlation, including differences in the institutions and industries that developed in areas with large African American populations. Prior work has argued that segregation has harmful effects on disadvantaged individuals through various channels: reducing exposure to successful peers and role models, decreasing funding for local public goods such as schools, or hampering access to nearby jobs (e.g., Massey and Denton, 1993; Wilson, 1987). Specifically, segregation may diminish upward mobility by spurring a spatial mismatch in access to jobs (Kain, 1968; Kasarda, 1989; Wilson, 1997). Chetty et al. (2014b) confirm that areas with less sprawl (shorter commutes) have significantly higher rates of upward mobility. Moreover, Chetty et al. (2014b) find that segregation of poverty has a strong negative association with upward mobility, whereas segregation of affluence does not. Isolation of low-income families (rather than the isolation of the rich) may be most detrimental to low-income children's prospects of moving up in the income distribution.

Third, quantitative and qualitative public investments in education: Chetty et al. (2014b) find a positive correlation between public school expenditures and upward mobility, but the correlation is not as strong or robust as the latter's association with different inequality measures or segregation. Ichino, Karabarbounis, and Moretti (2011) correlate the estimated IGE of income in 10 countries (Denmark, Finland, Canada, Sweden, Germany, France, United States, United Kingdom, Spain, and Australia) with public expenditure on education and find it equals −0.54. They report the correlation is even stronger when they focus on public expenditure on primary education. Mayer and Lopoo (2008) use the Population Study of Income Dynamics (PSID) and find that intergenerational earnings elasticities are higher in US states with low per-child spending compared to higher-spending ones. These estimates are robust to the inclusion of fixed effects for the state the child resided in at age 15 (identification then comes from changes over time in state-level spending). This study is interesting because it is not reliant on cross-sectional variation across states. Chetty et al. (2014b) also find a strong negative correlation of class size, income-adjusted test scores, and dropout rates with upward mobility. These results are consistent with the hypothesis that the quality of schools – as judged by outputs rather than inputs – plays a role in upward mobility. At a minimum, these findings strengthen the view that much of the difference in intergenerational income mobility across areas emerges while children are relatively young. That said, even public investments in education could be 'unequalizing'. For example, the children of affluent parents go to the top public (or private) schools, whereas the children in poorer and remote communities go to schools with teachers who are less well-trained (or may be absent) and the schools lack internet access. In short, there is a qualitative issue too.

Fourth, there is the startling stability of GNI capture by the 'middle'. Palma (2006, 2011, 2013, 2014) highlights empirically that the share of gross national income (GNI) accrued by those neither at the top nor the bottom of the distribution but instead in the 'middle' (the fifth to ninth deciles) remains stable over time and across countries at about 50 per cent of GNI (see also Cobham, Schlogl, and Sumner, 2016). Accordingly, changes in inequality tend to stem from a reallocation of the GNI share going to the wealthiest 10 per cent and poorest 40 per cent of the population – in Palma's words, to the 'heterogenous tails' since their GNI share varies across countries. In fact, in most cases where data are available, changes in the national Gini have been induced by changes in the GNI share accrued by the richest decile. Palma (2011, p. 102) describes this phenomenon of the homogenous middles as such:

> It seems that a schoolteacher, a junior or mid-level civil servant, a young professional (other than economics graduates working in financial markets), a skilled worker, middle manager, or a taxi driver who owns his or her own car, all tend to earn the same income across the world – as long as their incomes are normalised by the income per capita of the respective country.

Palma remarks significant differences between the GNI share and thus the income and consumption levels of decile 9 versus decile 10. He also identifies differences in the GNI share and thus income/expenditure patterns of those in the middle, implying there is a lower-middle income group comprising the 20 per cent above the poor, or deciles 5 and 6, and an upper middle encompassing the 30 per cent below the rich, that is, deciles 7 to 9. Palma (2014) describes a 'sub-optimal equilibrium' in certain Latin American middle-income countries (MICs) that manifests itself in high inequality but little social unrest since deciles 5 to 9 still benefit, for example, from cheap availability of services such as domestic maids, while the poorest profit from growing employment opportunities in the service sector despite low wages. Consequently, in these contexts, high inequality prevails alongside little growth and low unemployment. In turn, high inequality accompanied by high unemployment, as is the case in, for example, South Africa, tends to spur social instability. Palma (2014, pp. 28–9) characterises the equilibrium of high inequality, low unemployment, and little growth as such:

> It keeps the rich blissful (huge rewards with few market 'compulsions'); it allows the middle and upper middle groups to have access to a particularity large variety of cheap services; and it does at least provide high levels of employment for the bottom 40 per cent . . . jobs may be precarious, mostly at minimum wages . . . and in activities with little or no potential for long-term productivity growth, but at least they are jobs and there are plenty of them.

Finally, cross-cutting these set of issues is the question of economic dualism in developing countries (See discussion in Sumner, 2021). For Lewis (1954, 1955, 1958, 1969, 1972, 1976, 1979) and many others, notably, the more pessimistic, Furtado (1964 [1961], 1983 [1978]), developing countries are characterised by the existence of a backward/traditional/pre-capitalist sector alongside a modern/capitalist sector. The pre-capitalist sector acts as labour reserve and keeps wages low across the economy. For Lewis the transfer of labour from the traditional to the modern sector leads to capital accumulation, as profits are reinvested, and wages stay low. In contrast, for Furtado, the process reproduces the two sectors or 'structural duality' and leads to stagnation as the rate of profit falls because the internal markets size constrains economies of scale in the production of intermediate and capital goods. Furtado viewed industrialisation in Latin America – and developing countries more generally – as a process of stagnation and polarisation. He specifically argued that industrialisation polarises, stratifies, and segments labour markets into one for formal employment of better paid, middle-class people and one for informal employment of less well paid, poorer people. This bifurcation means that Furtado questioned whether the Lewis turning point exists. In short, the pool of surplus labour is reproduced and the Lewisian turning point delayed indefinitely. If one takes the Furtado position, then dualism will inevitably lead to lower social mobility in a swollen traditional sector. Even if one takes the more optimistic Lewisian position the transfer of labour from traditional to modern would need to be at a fair pace to ensure the parents born in the traditional sector transferred so their children grew up employed in the modern sector. In light of the fact that the earlier empirical pattern of structural transformation found by Baymul and Sen (2020) of agriculture to manufacturing has become a labour transition is from agriculture to low productivity services it would seem Lewis' optimism has been replaced with Furtado's pessimism with consequences for social mobility.

In sum, the relationship between mobility, inequality and development – or the reproduction of inequality – is determined by a set of factors as illustrated by empirical studies. Specifically, factors that boost future earnings of children of the 'privileged' class – for example, schooling quality – and issues disadvantaging those in the 'trapped' poorer class – for instance, segregation. Further, reinforcing these mechanisms is the economic dualism evident in developing countries. In the following section we conclude.

8 Conclusion

In conclusion, this Element has surveyed the area of mobility with reference to developing countries in particular. This contribution of this Element has been to review the concepts, measures and empirical estimate of studies; to discuss how mobility relates to income inequality; to present a new estimate for a developing country, namely Indonesia; and to discuss an empirical-based theoretical framework on the determinants of mobility.

To recap, in Section 2 we surveyed the field of mobility studies. Section 3 outlined approaches to conceptualise and measure mobility. Sections 4 and 5 reviewed empirical studies investigating mobility in developed countries and developing countries. We added our new estimate for Indonesia. In Sections 6 and 7 we respectively discussed the Great Gatsby Curve and outlined a theoretical framework based on empirical studies.

We conclude returning to the Great Gatsby Curve and its application in the Global South. In general, developed countries exhibit higher mobility and less inequality, than, in general, for developing countries. Furthermore, at any given level of income inequality the intergenerational elasticity of income is likely to be higher (and thus mobility worse) in a developing country than in a developed country. This implies – with more research needed – that a more meaningful reduction of inequality – of outcomes and of opportunities – via more substantial redistribution is likely to be necessary for developing countries than developed countries to achieve fairer societies.

References

Antman, F., & McKenzie, D. (2007). Poverty Traps and Nonlinear Income Dynamics with Measurement Error and Individual Heterogeneity. *The Journal of Development Studies*, *43*(6), 1057–83. https://doi.org/10.1080/00220380 701466567.

Atkinson, A. B., & Morelli, S. (2014). *Chartbook of Economic Inequality.* ECINEQ Working Paper No. 324.

Atkinson, A. (1981). On Intergenerational Income Mobility in Britain. *Journal of Post Keynesian Economics*, *3*(2), 194–218.

Atkinson, A., Trinder, CG., Maynard, AK. (1978) Evidence on intergenerational income mobility in Britain Economics Letters, 1(4), 383–388

Bane, M. J., & Ellwood, D. T. (1986). Slipping Into and Out of Poverty: The Dynamics of Spells. *The Journal of Human Resources*, *21*(1), 1–23. https://doi.org/10.2307/145955.

Barrett, C. B., & Carter, M. R. (2013). The Economics of Poverty Traps and Persistent Poverty: Empirical and Policy Implications. *The Journal of Development Studies*, *49*(7), 976–90. https://doi.org/10.1080/00220388.2013 .785527.

Baymul, C., & Sen, K. (2020). Was Kuznets Right? New Evidence on the Relationship between Structural Transformation and Inequality. *Journal of Development Studies*, *56*(9), 1643–62.

Becker, G. S., Kominers, S. D., Murphy, K. M., & Spenkuch, J. L. (2018). A Theory of Intergenerational Mobility. *Journal of Political Economy*, *126*(S1), 7–25.

Becker, G. S., & Tomes, N. (1979). An Equilibrium Theory of the Distribution of Income and Intergerational Mobility. *Journal of Political Economy*, *87*(6), 1153–89.

Becker, G. S., & Tomes, N. (1986). Human Capital and the Rise and Fall of Families. *Journal of Labor Economics*, *4*(3), S1–S39.

Bhattacharya, D., & Mazumder, B. (2011). A Nonparametric Analysis of Black-White Differences in Intergenerational Income Mobility in the United States. *Quantitative Economics*, *2*(3), 335–79. https://doi.org/10.3982/QE69.

Björklund, B. A., & Jäntti, M. (1997). Intergenerational Income Mobility in Sweden Compared to the United States. *The American Economic Review*, 168, *87*(5), 1009–18.

Björklund, A., Roine, J., & Waldenström, D. (2012). Intergenerational Top Income Mobility in Sweden: Capitalist Dynasties in the Land of Equal

Opportunity? *Journal of Public Economics*, *96*(5–6), 474–84. https://doi .org/10.1016/j.jpubeco.2012.02.003.

Black, S., & Devereux, P. (2010). *Recent Developments in Intergenerational Mobility.* NBER Working Paper No. 15889.

Black, S. E., & Devereux, P. J. (2011). Recent Developments in Intergenerational Mobility. In D. Card & O. Ashenfelter (Eds.), *Handbook of Labor Economics* (1st ed., Vol. 4B, pp. 1487–541). Elsevier.

Blanden, J. (2009). *How Much Can We Learn from International Comparisons of Intergenerational Mobility?* Centre for Economics of Education Discussion Paper No. 111.

Bratberg, E., Davis, J., Mazumder, B. et al. (2017). A Comparison of Intergenerational Mobility Curves in Germany, Norway, Sweden, and the US. *Scandinavian Journal of Economics*, *119*(1), 72–101. https://doi.org/10.1111/ sjoe.12197.

Bratsberg, B., Røed, K., Raaum, O. et al. (2007). Nonlinearities in intergenerational earnings mobility. *The Economic Journal*, *117*, C72–C92.

Chetty, R., Friedman, J. N., Saez, E., Turner, N., & Yagan, D. (2017). *Mobility Report Cards: The Role of Colleges in Intergenerational Mobility.* NBER Working Paper No. 23618.

Chetty, R., Grusky, D., Herll, M. et al. (2017). The Fading American Dream: Trends in Absolute Income Mobility since 1940. *Science*, *356*, 398–406.

Chetty, R., Hendren, N., & Katz, L. F. (2016). *The Effects of Exposure to Better Neighborhoods on Children: New Evidence from the Moving to Opportunity Experiment.* NBER Working Paper No. 23002.

Chetty, R., Hendren, N., Kline, P., & Saez, E. (2014a). Where Is the Land of Opportunity? The Geography of Intergenerational Mobility in the United States. *Quarterly Journal of Economics*, *129*(4), 1553–623.

Chetty, R., Hendren, N., Kline, P., Saez, E., & Turner, N. (2014b). Is the United States Still a Land of Opportunity? Recent Trends in Intergenerational Mobility. *American Economic Review: Papers and Proceedings*, *104*(5), 141–7.

Cobham, A., Schlogl, L., & Sumner, A. (2016). Inequality and the Tails: The Palma Proposition and Ratio. *Global Policy*, *7*(1), 25–36.

Corak, M. (2006). *Do Poor Children Become Poor Adults? Lessons from a Cross Country Comparison of Generational Income Mobility.* IZA Discussion Paper No. 1993.

Corak, M. (2013). Income Inequality, Equality of Opportunity, and Intergenerational Mobility. *Journal of Economic Perspectives*, *27*(3), 79–102. https://doi.org/ 10.1257/jep.27.3.79.

Corak, M., Lindquist, M. J., & Mazumder, B. (2014). A Comparison of Upward and Downward Intergenerational Mobility in Canada, Sweden and the United

States. *Labour Economics, 30,* 185–200. https://doi.org/10.1016/j.labeco.2014 .03.013.

Couch, K. A., & Dunn, T. A. (1997). Intergenerational Correlations in Labor Market Status: A Comparison of the United States and Germany. *The Journal of Human Resources, 32*(1), 210–32.

Dartanto, T., Moeis, F. R., & Otsubo, S. (2019). Intragenerational Economic Mobility in Indonesia: A Transition from Poverty to Middle Class during 1993–2014. *Bulletin of Indonesian Economic Studies, 56*(3), 1–57. https:// doi.org/10.1080/00074918.2019.1657795.

Dearden, L., Machin, S., & Reed, H. (1997). Intergenerational Mobility in Britain. *The Economic Journal, 107*(440), 47–66. https://doi.org/10.1111/1468-0297 .00141.

Deng, Q., Gustafsson, B., & Shi, L. (2013). Intergenerational Income Persistence in Urban China. *Review of Income and Wealth, 59*(3), 416–36.

Dercon, S., & Shapiro, J. (2007). *Moving On, Staying Behind, Getting Lost: Lessons on Poverty Mobility from Longitudinal Data.* GPRG Working Paper No. 075.

DiPrete, T. (2020). The Impact of Inequality on Intergenerational Mobility. *Annual Review of Sociology, 46,* 379–98.

Durlauf, S., Kourtellos, A., & Ming Tan, C. (2021). The Great Gastby Curve. *Annual Review of Economics, 14,* 571–605.

Emran, M. S., Greene, W., & Shilpi, F. (2018). When Measure Matters: Coresidency, Truncation Bias, and Intergenerational Mobility in Developing Countries. *Journal of Human Resources, 53*(3), 589–607.

Essama-Nssah, B., & Lambert, P. J. (2015). Influence Functions for Policy Impact Analysis. In *Inequality, Mobility and Segregation: Essays in Honor of Jacques Silber* (pp. 135–59). Emerald Group. https://doi.org/10.1108/ S1049-2585(2012)0000020009.

Essama-Nssah, B., & Lambert, P. J. (2016). Counterfactual Decomposition of Pro-poorness Using Influence Functions. *Journal of Human Development and Capabilities, 17*(1), 74–92. https://doi.org/10.1080/19452829.2015.1115392.

Ferreira, S. G., & Veloso, F. A. (2006). Intergenerational Mobility of Wages in Brazil. *Brazilian Review of Econometrics, 26*(2), 181–211. https://doi.org/ 10.12660/bre.v26n22006.1576.

Fields, G. (2005). *The Many Facets of Economic Mobility.* Department of Economics, Cornell University. www.ilr.cornell.edu/directory/gsf2/ downloads/Fields,ManyFacetsJul05.pdf.

Fields, G. (2021). Exploring Concepts of Social Mobility. In V. Iversen, A. Krishna, & K. Sen (Eds.), *Social Mobility in Developing Countries: Concepts, Methods, and Determinants* (pp. 54–74). Oxford University Press.

Fields, G. S., & Ok, E. A. (1999). The Measurement of Income Mobility: An Introduction to the Literature. In J. Silber (Ed.), *Handbook of Income Inequality Measurement* (2nd ed., pp. 557–98). Springer Science+Business Media.

Firpo, S., Fortin, N. M., & Lemieux, T. (2009). Unconditional Quantile Regressions. *Econometrica*, *77*(3), 953–73. https://doi.org/10.3982/ECTA6822.

Foster, J. E. (2009). A Class of Chronic Poverty Measures. In T. Addison, D. Hulme, & R. Kanbur (Eds.), *Poverty Dynamics: Interdisciplinary Perspectives* (pp. 59–76). Oxford University Press. https://doi.org/10.1093/acprof:oso/9780199557547.003.0003.

Foster, J. E., & Santos, M. E. (2014). Measuring Chronic Poverty. In G. Betti & A. Lemmi (Eds.), *Poverty and Social Exclusion: New Methods of Analysis* (pp. 143–65). Routledge. https://doi.org/10.1080/1360081032000111698.

Furtado, C. (1964 [1961]). *Development and Underdevelopment*. University of California Press.

Furtado, C. (1983 [1978]). *Accumulation and Development: The Logic of Industrial Civilization*. Martin Robertson.

Galton, F. (1886). Regression Towards Mediocrity in Hereditary Stature. *The Journal of the Anthropological Institute of Great Britain and Ireland*, *15*, 246–63.

Glass, D. V. (1954). *Social Mobility in Britain*. Routledge.

Grawe, N. D. (2001). *Intergenerational Mobility in the U.S. and Abroad: Quantile and Mean Regression Measures*. Paris School of Economics. http://piketty.pse.ens.fr/files/Grawe2001.pdf.

Grawe, N. D. (2004). Intergenerational Mobility for Whom? The Experience of High- and Low-Earning Sons in International Perspective. In M. Corak (Ed.), *Generational Income Mobility in North America and Europe* (pp. 58–89). Cambridge University Press.

Gregg, P., Macmillan, L., & Vittori, C. (2019). Intergenerational Income Mobility: Access to Top Jobs, the Low-Pay No-Pay Cycle and the Role of Education in a Common Framework. *Journal of Population Economics*, *32*, 501–28.

Heckley, G., Gerdtham, U. G., & Kjellsson, G. (2016). A General Method for Decomposing the Causes of Socioeconomic Inequality in Health. *Journal of Health Economics*, *48*, 89–106. https://doi.org/10.1016/j.jhealeco.2016.03.006.

Himanshu, & Lanjouw, P. (2021). The State of Knowledge about Social Mobility in the Developing World. In V. Iversen, A. Krishna, & K. Sen (Eds.), *Social Mobility in Developing Countries: Concepts, Methods, and Determinants* (pp. 3–32). Oxford University Press.

Ichino, A., Karabarbounis, L., & Moretti, E. (2011). The Political Economy of Intergenerational Income Mobility. *Economic Inquiry, 49*(1), 47–69. https://doi.org/10.1111/j.1465-7295.2010.00320.x.

Iversen, V. (2021). Social Mobility in Developing Countries: Directions for Research Practice, Knowledge Gaps, and Policy Support. In V. Iversen, A. Krishna, & K. Sen (Eds.), *Social Mobility in Developing Countries: Concepts, Methods, and Determinants* (pp. 451–60). Oxford University Press.

Iversen, V., Krishna, A., & Sen, K. (Eds.). (2021a). *Social Mobility in Developing Countries: Concepts, Methods, and Determinants*. Oxford University Press.

Iversen, V., Krishna, A., & Sen, K. (2021b). Social Mobility in Developing Countries: Directions for Research Practice, Knowledge Gaps, and Policy Support. In V. Iversen, A. Krishna, & K. Sen (Eds.), *Social Mobility in Developing Countries: Concepts, Methods, and Determinants*. Oxford University Press.

Iversen, V., Krishna, A., & Sen, K. (2021c). The State of Knowledge about Social Mobility in the Developing World. In V. Iversen, A. Krishna, & K. Sen (Eds.), *Social Mobility in Developing Countries: Concepts, Methods, and Determinants* (pp. 3–34). Oxford University Press.

Jäntti, M., & Jenkins, S. P. (2015). Income Mobility. In A. B. Atkinson & F. Bourguignon (Eds.), *Handbook of Income Distribution* (1st ed., Vol. 2A, pp. 807–936). Elsevier.

Jäntti, M., Naylor, R., Österbacka, E. et al. (2006). *American Exceptionalism in a New Light: A Comparison of Intergenerational Earnings Mobility in the Nordic Countries, the United Kingdom and the United States*. IZA Discussion Paper No. 1938, pp. 1–40.

Kain, J. (1968). Housing Segregation, Negro Employment, and Metropolitan Decentralization. *The Quarterly Journal of Economics, 82*(2), 175–97.

Kanbur, R. (2021). In Praise of Snapshots. In V. Iversen, A. Krishna, & K. Sen (Eds.), *Social Mobility in Developing Countries: Concepts, Methods, and Determinants* (pp. 97–114). Oxford University Press.

Kasarda, J. (1989). The Ghetto Underclass: Social Science Perspectives. *The Annals of the American Academy of Political and Social Science, 501*, 26–47.

Khaldun, I. (1978). *The Muqaddimah*. Routledge & Kegan Paul.

Koenker, R., & Bassett, G. (1978). Regression Quantiles. *Econometrica, 46*(1), 33–50. https://doi.org/10.2307/1913643.

Kourtellos, A., Marr, C., & Tan, C. M. (2016). Robust Determinants of Intergenerational Mobility in the Land of Opportunity. *European Economic Review, 81*, 132–47. https://doi.org/10.1016/j.euroecorev.2015.07.008.

Krueger, A. (2012). *The Rise and Consequences of Inequality in the United States*. The Center for American Progress.

Krueger, A. B. (2013). *Land of Hope and Dreams: Rock and Roll, Economics and Rebuilding the Middle Class*. White House.

Lewis, W. A. (1954). Economic Development with Unlimited Supplies of Labour. *The Manchester School, 22*(2), 139–91.

Lewis, W. A. (1955). *The Theory of Economic Growth*. Richard D. Irwin.

Lewis, W. A. (1958). Employment Policy in an Underdeveloped Area. *Social and Economic Studies, 7*(3), 42–54.

Lewis, W. A. (1969). *Aspects of Tropical Trade, 1883–1965*. Almqvist and Wicksell.

Lewis, W. A. (1972). Reflections on Unlimited Labour. In L. E. diMarco (Ed.), *International Economics and Development: Essays in Honour of Raoul Prebisch* (pp. 75–96). Academic Press.

Lewis, W. A. (1976). Development and Distribution. In A. Cairncross & M. Puri (Eds.), *Employment, Income Distribution and Development Strategy: Essays in Honour of Hans Singer* (pp. 26–42). Macmillan.

Lewis, W. A. (1979). The Dual Economy Revisited. *The Manchester School, 47* (3), 211–29.

Lillard, L. A., & Willis, R. J. (1978). Dynamic Aspects of Earning Mobility. *Econometrica, 46*(5), 985–1012. https://doi.org/10.2307/1911432.

Massey, D. S., & Denton, N. A. (1993). *American Apartheid: Segregation and the Making of the Underclass*. Harvard University Press.

Mayer, S. E., & Lopoo, L. M. (2008). Government Spending and Intergenerational Mobility. *Journal of Public Economics, 92*, 139–58. https://doi.org/10.1016/j.jpubeco.2007.04.003.

Mckay, A., & Lawson, D. (2003). Assessing the Extent and Nature of Chronic Poverty in Low Income Countries: Issues and Evidence. *World Development, 31*(3), 425–39. https://doi.org/10.1016/S0305-750X(02)00221-8.

Mulligan, C. B. (1997). *Parental Priorities and Economic Inequality*. University of Chicago Press.

Narayan, A., Van der Weide, R., Cojocaru, A. et al. (2018). *Fair Progress? Economic Mobility Across Generations Around the World*. World Bank.

Neidhöfer, G., Serrano, J., & Gasparini, L. (2018). Educational Inequality and Intergenerational Mobility in Latin America: A New Database. *Journal of Development Economics, 134*, 329–49. https://doi.org/10.1016/j.jdeveco.2018.05.016.

Nybom, M., & Stuhler, J. (2015). *Biases in Standard Measures of Intergenerational Income Dependence*. IFAU Working Paper No. 13.

Nybom, M., & Stuhler, J. (2017). Biases in Standard Measures of Intergenerational Income Dependence. *Journal of Human Resources, 52*(3), 800–25.

Obama, B. (2011, December 7). *Full Text of Barack Obama's Speech in Osawatomie, Kansas*. The Guardian, www.theguardian.com/world/2011/dec/07/full-text-barack-obama-speech.

OECD. (2011). Special Focus: Inequality in Emerging Economies. In *Divided We Stand: Why Inequality Keeps Rising* (pp. 47–82).

Palma, J. G. (2006). *Globalizing Inequality: 'Centrifugal' and 'Centripetal' Forces at Work*. UNDESA Working Paper No. 35.

Palma, J. G. (2011). Homogeneous Middles vs. Heterogeneous Tails, and the End of the 'Inverted-U': The Share of the Rich Is What It's All about. *Development and Change, 42*(1), 87–153.

Palma, G. (2013). *Has the Income Share of the Middle and Upper-Middle Been Stable over Time, or Is Its Current Homogeneity Across the World the Outcome of a Process of Convergence? The 'Palma Ratio' Revisited*. Cambridge Working Papers in Economics No. 1437.

Palma, G. (2014). Has the Income Share of the Middle and Upper-Middle Been Stable around the '50/50 Rule', or Has It Converged towards that Level? The 'Palma Ratio' Revisited. *Development and Change, 45*(6), 1416–48.

Palomino, J. C., Marrero, G. A., & Rodríguez, J. G. (2018). One Size Doesn't Fit All: A Quantile Analysis of Intergenerational Income Mobility in the U.S. (1980–2010). *Journal of Economic Inequality, 16*(3), 347–67. https://doi.org/10.1007/s10888-017-9372-8.

Pekkarinen, T., Salvanes, K. G., & Sarvimäki, M. (2017). The Evolution of Social Mobility: Norway during the Twentieth Century. *Scandinavian Journal of Economics, 119*(1), 5–33. https://doi.org/10.1111/sjoe.12205.

The Pew Charitable Trusts. (2012). *Pursuing the American Dream: Economic Mobility Across Generations*.

Piketty, T. (1995). Social Mobility and Redistributive Politics. *The Quarterly Journal of Economics, 110*(3), 551–84.

Piketty, T. (2000). Theories of Persistent Inequality and Intergenerational Mobility. In A. B. Atkinson & F. Bourguignon (Eds.), *Handbook of Income Distribution* (Vol. 1, pp. 429–76). Elsevier. https://doi.org/10.1016/S1874-5792(05)80001-1.

Piraino, P. (2021). Drivers of Mobility in the Global South. In V. Iversen, A. Krishna, & K. Sen (Eds.), *Social Mobility in Developing Countries: Concepts, Methods, and Determinants* (pp. 35–53). Oxford University Press.

Ravallion, M. (1988). Expected Poverty under Risk-Induced Welfare Variability. *The Economic Journal, 98*(393), 1171–82. https://doi.org/10.2307/2233725.

Rodgers, J. R., & Rodgers, J. L. (1993). Chronic Poverty in the United States. *The Journal of Human Resources*, *28*(1), 25–54. https://doi.org/10.2307/146087.

Roemer, J. (1998). *Equality of Opportunity*. Harvard University Press.

Sakri, D. (2019). *Intergenerational Income Mobility in Indonesia, 1993–2014*. King's College London. https://kclpure.kcl.ac.uk/portal/files/130571264/2020_Sakri_Diding_1573546_ethesis.pdf.

Sakri, D., Sumner, A., & Yusuf, A. A. (2022). *Whose Intergenerational Mobility? A New Set of Estimates for Indonesia by Gender, Geography, and Generation*. WIDER Working Paper No. 12.

Savegnago, M. (2016). Igmobil: A Command for Intergenerational Mobility Analysis in Stata. *The Stata Journal: Promoting Communications on Statistics and Stata*, *16*(2), 386–402. https://doi.org/10.1177/1536867x1601600207.

Shorrocks, A. (1978). Income Inequality and Income Mobility. *Journal of Economic Theory*, *19*(2), 376–93. https://doi.org/10.1016/0022-0531(78)90101-1.

Solon, G. (1999). Intergenerational Mobility in the Labor Market. In O. Ashenfelter & D. Card (Eds.), *Handbook of Labor Economics* (1st ed., pp. 1761–800). Elsevier.

Solon, G. (2004). A Model of Intergenerational Mobility Variation Over Time and Place. In M.Corak (Ed.), *Generational Income Mobility in North America and Europe* (pp. 1–13). Cambridge University Press.

Solon, G., Corcoran, M., Gordon, R., & Laren, D. (1991). A Longitudinal Analysis of Sibling Correlations in Economic Status. *Journal of Human Resources*, *26*(3), 509–34.

Sorkin, P. (1927). *Social Mobility*. Harper.

Stevens, A. H. (1999). Climbing Out of Poverty, Falling Back In: Measuring the Persistence of Poverty Over Multiple Spells. *The Journal of Human Resources*, *34*(3), 557–88. https://doi.org/10.2307/146380.

Strauss, J., Witoelar, F., & Sikoki, B. (2016). *The Fifth Wave of the Indonesia Family Life Survey: Overview and Field Report* (Vol. 1). Paper No. WR-1143/1-NIA/NICHD. www.rand.org/labor/FLS/IFLS/download.html.

Sumner, A. (2021). *Deindustrialisation, Distribution and Development: Structural Change in the Global South*. Oxford University Press.

UNU-WIDER. (2021). *WIID – World Income Inequality Database*.

Van der Weide, R., Lakner, C., Mahler, D. G., Narayan, A., & Ramasubbaiah, R. (2021). *Intergenerational Mobility around the World*. Policy Research Working Paper No. 9707.

Wilson, W. (1987). *The Truly Disadvantaged*. University of Chicago Press.

Wilson, W. J. (1997). *When Work Disappears*. Vintage Books.

The World Bank. (2015). *Indonesia's Rising Divide.*

The World Bank. (2018). *Global Database on Intergenerational Mobility.*

Yusuf, A., Sumner, A., & Rum, I. (2014). Twenty Years of Expenditure Inequality in Indonesia, 1993–2013. *Bulletin of Indonesian Economic Studies*, *50*(2), 243–54.

Zimmerman, D. J. (1992). Regression Toward Mediocrity in Economic Stature. *American Economic Review*, *82*(3), 409–29.

Cambridge Elements ☰

Development Economics

Series Editor-in-Chief
Kunal Sen
UNU-WIDER, and University of Manchester

Kunal Sen, UNU-WIDER Director, is Editor-in-Chief of the Cambridge Elements in Development Economics series. Professor Sen has over three decades of experience in academic and applied development economics research, and has carried out extensive work on international finance, the political economy of inclusive growth, the dynamics of poverty, social exclusion, female labour force participation, and the informal sector in developing economies. His research has focused on India, East Asia, and sub-Saharan Africa.

In addition to his work as Professor of Development Economics at the University of Manchester, Kunal has been the Joint Research Director of the Effective States and Inclusive Development (ESID) Research Centre, and a Research Fellow at the Institute for Labor Economics (IZA). He has also served in advisory roles with national governments and bilateral and multilateral development agencies, including the UK's Department for International Development, Asian Development Bank, and the International Development Research Centre.

Thematic Editors
Tony Addison
University of Copenhagen, and UNU-WIDER

Tony Addison is a Professor of Economics in the University of Copenhagen's Development Economics Research Group. He is also a Non-Resident Senior Research Fellow at UNU-WIDER, Helsinki, where he was previously the Chief Economist-Deputy Director. In addition, he is Professor of Development Studies at the University of Manchester. His research interests focus on the extractive industries, energy transition, and macroeconomic policy for development.

Chris Barret
Johnson College of Business, Cornell University

Chris Barrett is an agricultural and development economist at Cornell University. He is the Stephen B. and Janice G. Ashley Professor of Applied Economics and Management; and International Professor of Agriculture at the Charles H. Dyson School of Applied Economics and Management. He is also an elected Fellow of the American Association for the Advancement of Science, the Agricultural and Applied Economics Association, and the African Association of Agricultural Economists.

Carlos Gradín
UNU-WIDER, and University of Vigo

Carlos Gradín is a UNU-WIDER Research Fellow, and a professor of applied economics at the University of Vigo (on leave). His main research interest is the study of inequalities, with special attention to those that exist between population groups (e.g., by race or sex). His publications have contributed to improving the empirical evidence in developing and developed countries, as well as globally, and to improving the available data and methods used.

Rachel M. Gisselquist
UNU-WIDER

Rachel M. Gisselquist is a Senior Research Fellow and member of the Senior Management Team of UNU-WIDER. She specializes in the comparative politics of developing countries, with particular attention to issues of inequality, ethnic and identity politics, foreign aid and state building, democracy and governance, and sub-Saharan African politics. Dr Gisselquist has edited a dozen collections in these areas, and her articles are published in a range of leading journals.

Shareen Joshi
Georgetown University

Shareen Joshi is an Associate Professor of International Development at Georgetown University's School of Foreign Service in the United States. Her research focuses on issues of inequality, human capital investment and grassroots collective action in South Asia. Her work has been published in the fields of development economics, population studies, environmental studies and gender studies.

Patricia Justino
Senior Research Fellow, UNU-WIDER, and IDS – UK

Patricia Justino is a Senior Research Fellow at UNU-WIDER and Professorial Fellow at the Institute of Development Studies (IDS) (on leave). Her research focuses on the relationship between political violence, governance and development outcomes. She has published widely in the fields of development economics and political economy and is the co-founder and co-director of the Households in Conflict Network (HiCN).

Marinella Leone
University of Pavia

Marinella Leone is an assistant professor at the Department of Economics and Management, University of Pavia, Italy. She is an applied development economist. Her more recent research focuses on the study of early child development parenting programmes, on education, and gender-based violence. In previous research she investigated the short-, long-term and intergenerational impact of conflicts on health, education and domestic violence. She has published in top journals in economics and development economics.

Jukka Pirttilä
University of Helsinki, and UNU-WIDER

Jukka Pirttilä is Professor of Public Economics at the University of Helsinki and VATT Institute for Economic Research. He is also a Non-Resident Senior Research Fellow at UNU-WIDER. His research focuses on tax policy, especially for developing countries. He is a co-principal investigator at the Finnish Centre of Excellence in Tax Systems Research.

Andy Sumner
King's College London, and UNU-WIDER

Andy Sumner is Professor of International Development at King's College London; a Non-Resident Senior Fellow at UNU-WIDER and a Fellow of the Academy of Social Sciences. He has published extensively in the areas of poverty, inequality, and economic development.

About the Series

Cambridge Elements in Development Economics is led by UNU-WIDER in partnership with Cambridge University Press. The series publishes authoritative studies on important topics in the field covering both micro and macro aspects of development economics.

United Nations University World Institute for Development Economics Research

United Nations University World Institute for Development Economics Research (UNU-WIDER) provides economic analysis and policy advice aiming to promote sustainable and equitable development for all. The institute began operations in 1985 in Helsinki, Finland, as the first research centre of the United Nations University. Today, it is one of the world's leading development economics think tanks, working closely with a vast network of academic researchers and policy makers, mostly based in the Global South.

UNITED NATIONS
UNIVERSITY
UNU-WIDER

Cambridge Elements ≡

Development Economics

Printed in the United States
by Baker & Taylor Publisher Services